Nevada Real Estate EXAM PREP

The SMART Guide to Passing

Harry V. Eastlick

CENGAGE Learning™

Australia • Brazil • Japan • Korea • Mexico • Singapore • Spain • United Kingdom • United States

CENGAGE Learning™

Nevada Real Estate Exam Prep

Vice President of Editorial, Business: Jack W. Calhoun

Vice President/Editor-in-Chief:

Acquisitions Editor: Sara Glassmeyer

Developmental Editor: Arlin Kauffman

Editorial Assistant: Michelle Melfi

Senior Marketing and Sales Manager: Mark Linton

Technology Project Manager: Matt McKinney

Senior Manufacturing Buyer: Charlene Taylor

Production Service: PrePress PMG

Art Director: Pamela Galbreath

Library of Congress Control Number: 2009934430
ISBN-13: 978-0-324-64948-2
ISBN-10: 0-324-64948-7

Cengage Learning
5191 Natorp Boulevard
Mason, OH 45040
USA

Cengage Learning products are represented in Canada by Nelson Education, Ltd.

Printed in the United States of America
1 2 3 4 5 6 7 13 12 11 10 09

Introduction

Additional exposure to the material and repetition will improve your confidence and help alleviate "exam anxiety." The more you know, the less stress you will have when taking the test. There is no magic wand or "smart pill" you can take, but if you follow these guidelines, we think you will be successful.

General Study Hints

Use questions in your book more than once. Write your answers on a separate sheet of paper. This will make scoring easier as you compare your answers with the answer key in the back of the booklet, and leave the questions unmarked for additional "practice" retakes. This will also work with your regular textbook and any other practice exams you might decide to use.

Practice taking timed tests. Duplicate the testing situation by practicing the questions under pressure. This is one of the best ways to overcome exam anxiety. Based on the time allowed on the state examination, your goal should be to complete 50 questions per hour. Missed items quickly pinpoint your weak areas and help focus your attention on them for additional study.

Research wrong answers. First, carefully read the explanation in the answer key. Determine why the correct answer is correct and the other "distracters" are not. Try not to memorize individual questions, as this may cause you to miss subtle wording differences on the exam, thereby causing you to answer incorrectly. You need to concentrate on concepts, not exact phrasing.

Pace your studying. Immediately test yourself after class discussion. Look up wrong answers. Remember that last-minute cramming before a final exam or the state licensing exam may cause you to panic when confronted with difficult material or to become overly tired during the exam. Do not get behind in your studying; it is difficult to catch up.

Limit your study time. Most people more easily recall the first and last part of whatever they study, while the middle material becomes a little muddled. It is better to study for 10 to 20 minutes with breaks rather than for a solid hour.

Get a good night's sleep before the test. A proper amount of sleep will help you think more clearly and avoid errors from just being tired. Staying up all night will just make you tired and often more confused.

Know where you are going. If you are going to a test site in another town, know how to get there and give yourself lots of extra time. Do not add to your frustration by being late!

Know the testing rules. Review your examination guide to be sure you know how you will be tested and the general process. There are generally a few sample questions in the guide, as well as a list of content to be tested. There should also be a chart of how many questions will be asked in each general category.

Last-minute study. Your last-minute study should include definitions from your regular text for the national portion and the key point review for the Pennsylvania portion from this booklet. If you struggle with a given topic, don't waste time trying to master it at the very end. Move on and review the material with which you are more familiar.

If you are just beginning your class, try these additional tips:

Read the assigned material BEFORE class. If you are in a classroom setting, then the lecture should help reinforce what you have read. Highlight what you think are important points and jot down any questions you might need to ask. Don't highlight everything in your book! Hold your questions until the topic is completed as your question may be answered during the lecture. If ever unsure about asking, speak with the instructor during a break.

Participate, don't just talk. Instructors enjoy well-asked questions that give them an opportunity to "teach." However, no one enjoys a classroom where students are continually talking to each other or telling "war stories" that have little to do with the topic.

Organize your notes and handouts. Many students accumulate a lot of paper during a class, and it quickly becomes unorganized. Consider using a 3-ring binder or a folder with pockets to stay organized.

If you are in a classroom, be on time and always listen for instructions. Being late a time or two or daydreaming during class may mean missing a question or two. Those missed items could make the difference between passing and failing.

Test Taking Strategies

1. **Read the question.** Some students go so far as putting a huge "RTQ" on some scratch paper to remind them! It is imperative to know what is being asked. Look for words like NOT or EXCEPT or INCORRECT. In math questions, the numbers provided may be monthly, but the question is seeking an annual number. Make sure you understand the question before you look at the answers!
2. **Read the answers.** Go through the 4 choices. Look for ones that can be easily eliminated. Some students put "A B C D" on a sheet of paper for tougher questions and physically mark through incorrect answers as they are eliminated. If you can eliminate 2 answers, you now have a 50-50 chance, even if you have to guess! You might want to approach a multiple choice question as 4 separate True/False questions — you are looking for the True answer. On questions with two Yes and two No answers, be sure to read what follows the Yes and No, as that is usually the key to answering correctly.
3. **Review your answer.** When done, review by reading the question and the answer you picked, asking yourself, "Does this completed sentence make sense?" If it is a "story problem," put yourself in the story. Does the correct answer make common sense to you? On math problems, put the answer back into the formula. Also, is the answer logical? It wouldn't make sense for a $100,000 home to have annual real estate taxes of $50,000.
4. **Make sure you immediately record your answer.** Many students find that silly mistakes, such as recording "B" instead of "D" on their answer sheet, will cost them a point or two.
5. **Manage your time during the exam.** Go through the entire exam in order, answering the questions that come easily. If you are in doubt or do not know the answer, skip it and move on. Many students use 45–60 minutes to answer about 70% of the questions. This leaves plenty of time to focus on the remaining 30%. On computerized exams, there should be an indicator of how many questions have been answered and how much time is remaining.
6. **Manage your panic.** Better yet, don't panic! As you go through the exam the first time, remember that it is normal to leave about one out of four questions blank. When you come to a question that stumps you, remember that subsequent questions may jog your memory or provide answers to earlier questions; look for that help. Remember that you can miss 1 of every 4 questions and still pass.
7. **Stay comfortable and avoid stress.** Lean back in your chair and roll your neck occasionally. If necessary, get up and stretch or use the restroom. Staying comfortable will help you stay focused on the test itself. By the way, the small camera that may be on top of your computer station is there to take your picture for licensing — it is not there spying and constantly watching you as some students believe!
8. **Don't get stuck on any one question or problem.** Rather than dwell on a single problem, you could be answering several more questions to which you DO know the answer. Also, a later question may provide you with a clue or answer to the bypassed one. Get out of negative thinking and move on to the next question!

9. **Don't change an answer.** Unless you find an obvious mistake, such as an incorrectly recorded answer or misread question, do NOT change your original response. First instincts are correct more often than changed answers. Be 100% sure if you are going to make a change.
10. **Answer all questions.** Before handing your test in, or indicating on your computer that you are finished, be sure every question has an answer. If you are out of time, mark one answer for each randomly. It can only help your score.
11. **Additional information.** Nevada has subcontracted the duties of administering the real estate examinations to PSI Examination Services, Inc. PSI administers the exams to candidates via computer in testing centers located throughout Nevada.
    For questions relating to the PSI exam contact:
    PSI Examination Services
    Phone: 800-733-9267
    FAX: 818-247-3853
    Web: http://www.psiexams.com
12. **Congratulations — you've passed!** If so, you may want to let your instructor know. If you fail for some reason, before leaving the test site, write down topic areas that need more study. You may forget many of these if you wait until you get home.

State Exam Outline

[H2]Introduction

The State of Nevada salesperson and broker examinations contain 120 test questions that will be used to determine your score (80 national examination questions, plus 40 Nevada state-specific questions). The test may also contain 10 pretest questions mixed in throughout the examination. Because PSI Exams, Inc., who administers the Nevada examinations, provides a score to you immediately after you take the State of Nevada examination, they need to know how test questions perform before they are used to calculate your score. For this reason, PSI must pretest questions in order to evaluate question reliability. If a pretest question is included in your examination, it will not be counted in the calculation of your score. Pretest questions are not identified and you should answer all questions as if each counted toward your score. This will provide PSI with reliable evaluation of the questions. The following test outlines show the approximate number of questions on the state test for each major category.

National Test Outline

	Number of Questions Salesperson	Broker
I. Property Ownership	7	7
II. Land Use Controls and Regulations	7	7
III. Valuation and Market Analysis	7	6
IV. Financing	8	7
V. Laws of Agency	10	10
VI. Mandated Disclosures	6	7
VII. Contracts	10	10
VIII. Transfer of Property	7	6
IX. Practice of Real Estate	10	10
X. Real Estate Calculations	5	6
XI. Specialty Areas	3	4

Nevada State-Specific Outline

I. Commission Duties and Powers	4	4
II. Licensing	5	6
III. Standards of Conduct	16	13
IV. Agency/Brokerage	13	14
V. Special Topic	2	3

KEY POINT REVIEW

The following are key exam concepts that make a great final study guide for the real estate licensing exam. The key points are intentionally short and to the point to make them easier to understand and absorb. They are organized by the topic listed in the State Exam Outline.

I. Property Ownership

The key review points for Property Ownership are:

Classes of Property

1. Real property is defined as real estate that is owned or real estate plus the bundle of rights.
2. The bundle of rights, also called property rights, include the following:
    a. Control-Total control within the framework of the law.
    b. Possession-The right to have and to hold.
    c. Quiet and peaceful enjoyment-The right to use the property; no one has superior rights.
    d. Disposition-The right to sell, will, lease, barter or destroy.
    e. Encumbrance-The right to mortgage, grant easement, or burden title.
3. Personal property is moveable. Everything that is not real property is classified as personal property
4. Annual crops that require planting and cultivation are personal property and are called emblements
5. A fixture is formerly personal property that has become attached to real property and thus is now a part of the real property
6. Trade fixtures are items of personal property used in business that even if attached do not become real estate
7. A way to test whether an item is real property (a fixture) or personal property is to remember the acronym MARIA for:
    a. M = Method of Attachment
    b. A = Adaptability
    c. R = Relationship of Parties
    d. I = Intent of Annexor
    e. A = Agreement of Parties

Land Characteristics and Property Descriptions

8. Legal descriptions are essential for identifying any parcel of property in such a specific manner that the description is acceptable in a court of law. The three basic methods used in legal descriptions are:
    a. Metes and bounds description
    b. Rectangular survey (also called government survey)

c. Map and plat description (also known as lot and block description)

9. The three physical characteristics of real estate are:
   a. I = immobility- cannot be moved.
   b. I = indestructibility-durable; cannot be destroyed; just modified.
   c. U = uniqueness-no two parcel are the same-non-homogeneity

10. The four economic characteristics of real estate are:
    a. S = scarcity-available land in a given location may be limited.
    b. I = improvements-modifications made to a parcel of land cause an economic ripple effect on neighboring properties.
    c. F = fixed.investments- recovery of real estate investments generally takes 20 to 30 years.
    d. S = Situs- choice or preferences for a given area-considered the most important economic characteristic.
11. Land is defined as the Earth's surface, downward to the center of the Earth, upward to infinity, and including all things permanently attached by nature
12. Real estate is defined as the land plus man-made additions permanently attached to the Earth. These additions are called improvements, tenements and appurtenances

Encumbrances

13. An encumbrance is any claim, lien charge or liability attached to and binding on real property that may lessen the value, burden, obstruct, or impair the use of a property, but not necessarily prevent transfer of title. The two types of encumbrances are nonmonetary and monetary
14. Non-monetary encumbrances include:
    a. Deed restrictions
        1. Private limitations placed on land use at the time a subdivision is developed, or when a property owner sells the land.
        2. Included in each deed.
        3. When the deed restrictions uniformly affect all of the subdivision they are known as Covenants, Conditions, and Restrictions (CC&Rs).
        4. Enforced by court action; often brought by a homeowner's association.
    b. Easements – an interest that entitles one party to some limited use of another party's land. Types of easements include:

1. Appurtenant easements are attached to the land and if the property is sold, the easement is transferred to the new owner ("runs with the land").
    a. Tract over which easement runs equals servient tenement.
    b. Tract benefiting from the easement equal dominant tenement.
2. Personal easement in gross – a personal interest in using the land of another that cannot be transferred or assigned and terminates upon the death of the person to whom the easement was granted or upon the sale of the subject property.
3. Commercial easement in gross – a right to use granted to a public entity such as a railroad or utility that can be assigned or transferred.
4. Party wall easement – when a fence is built on the property line each person owns half of the fence on his or her property, and each owner has an easement on the other's property.
5. Methods used to create easements are:
    a. Express grant – usually executed by a separate deed.
    b. Reservation in a deed when ownership is transferred to a new buyer.
    c. Necessity – because it is illegal to sell landlocked land, an owner would have to grant an easement to allow ingress and egress to the property.
    d. Prescription – a method of acquiring an easement by continuous, open, hostile, and notorious use for a period of 10 years without the consent of the owner.
6. Easements may be terminated by agreement of the parties, a merger of the two properties, or by abandonment.
7. License is a personal privilege to use the land of another for a limited purpose, it can be revoked at any time and it usually is not transferable.

c. Encroachments – an intrusion upon another person's property without a right to use it; owner of the property being encroached upon has the right to force the removal of the encroachment and failure to do so may damage the owner's title.

15. Monetary encumbrances are called liens. A lien is a claim or charge against a property as security for the payment of a debt or obligation. Liens affect the title of the property involved and allow a creditor (lien holder) to force the sale of a property subject to the lien.

16. Liens can be classified as follows:
    a. Contractual – the parties enter into a contractual agreement, such as a mortgage or trust deed.
    b. Statutory – liens that are created by law, such as property taxes or special assessment taxes.
    c. Equitable – liens that occur when the courts declare that justice would be best served by the creation of a lien.
17. Liens can further be classified as follows:
    a. General liens – affect all property, both real and personal
    b. Specific liens – affect only one specific property
    c. Voluntary liens – created by voluntary actions of the individual
    d. Involuntary liens – created by law without action or consent of the individual
18. Liens with the highest priority are superior to junior liens. The higher-priority lien eliminates junior liens if the higher lien holder forecloses. Lien priority is determined as follows:
    a. Real property taxes always have the highest priority, followed by special assessments.
    b. Priority of other liens is determined by the order in which the lien is recorded except for mechanic's liens.
    c. Priority for mechanic's liens is determined by the date the work began.

Types of Ownership

19. Title is the right to ownership of property and the evidence of such rights
20. The two general classifications of estates in land are: freehold and leasehold
21. A freehold estate is a real property ownership estate of uncertain duration
22. A leasehold estate is less than a freehold and lasts for a certain duration of time
23. Freehold estates are classified as:
    a. Fee simple absolute
    b. Qualified or defeasible fee estates
    c. Conventional life estates
    d. Legal life estates
24. Fee simple absolute gives the owner the greatest interest possible and is of indefinite duration, but still subject to the government powers. The ownership interest is inheritable
25. Qualified fee estates are said to be defeasible because the ownership interest can be terminated if certain conditions are met or not met. There are three types of qualified fees:
    a. Fee simple determinable – the estate ends automatically on the current owner's failure to comply with the limitation established by a grantor in the deed without the need to go to court.

b. Fee simple on condition subsequent – the estate places conditions on the grantee and if the condition is violated, the grantor has a right to regain ownership, but only through legal action.

c. Fee simple conditional – an estate with a restriction to the right of inheritance, such as limiting the right of inheritance to a fixed line of succession. Fee simple conditional is not legal in Nevada

26. Conventional life estates are not inheritable and is a fee simple estate granted for the life of an individual, known as the life tenant. A property owner uses a deed that names the life tenant and specifies who will receive the property at the death of the life tenant. The interests of the parties who will receive the property are known as:

    a. Estate in reversion. The grantor of the life estate specifies by reservation in the deed that the property will be returned to the grantor, or his or her heirs at the time of the life tenant's death.

    b. Estate in remainder. The grantor states in the deed that upon the death of the life tenant, the property will go to a third person, known as the remainderman.

27. Conventional life estate-pur autre vie. A second type of life estate that differs only because the grantor names a life tenant, but the estate is based on the life of a person other than the life tenant. At death of the third person, the estate reverts to either the grantor or to a remainderman that has been specified in the deed by the grantor. An estate pur autre vie can be willed by the life tenant, but the estate is still limited by the life of third person

28. Legal life estates are created by statutory law and consist of the following:

    a. Dower- a life estate that a wife has in real estate of a deceased husband. Not applicable in Nevada.

    b. Curtesy- a life estate that a husband has in real estate of a deceased wife. Not applicable in Nevada.

    c. Homestead – the only legal life estate in Nevada. The homestead exemption protects the equity in an owner's primary residence up to $550,000. It protects the owner's equity against actions by general creditors, but not from actions by holders of voluntary specific liens on the primary residence.

29. Severalty is taking title as sole owner, wither as a natural person or a legal person

30. Concurrent ownership is a form of ownership in which two or more persons have an undivided interest in the same land. The five basic forms of concurrent ownership are:

    a. Tenants in common - each owner or part owner has an undivided interest and rights of possession of the entire parcel. The undivided rights exist even though there may be unequal shares. In Nevada, if two single people do not address how they choose to take title, they will automatically become tenants in common.

    b. Joint tenancy – also called joint tenancy with the right of survivorship (JTWROS). A type of ownership where in the case of a owner's death the survivor automatically acquires ownership of the property. A joint tenant owner can sell his or her interest separately. The last survivor owns all of the property in severalty. The four common-law unities that must be present to create JTWROS are:

1. Possession-equal rights for all
2. Interest-each has equal percent of ownership
3. Title-there is only one deed; all owners take title under one deed
4. Time-it must be created at the same time

c. Community property- each spouse has ownership of half of the marital property (both real and personal). For married couples in Nevada, title is automatically taken as community property, unless specifically stated otherwise in the deed. One spouse cannot separately sell his or her interest.

d. Community property with rights of survivorship (CPWROS) – A husband and wife may take title to property as CPWROS when the deed expressly state the right of survivorship is desired. The four common-law unities required to create a joint tenancy are not required. The surviving spouse will own the property in severalty.

e. Tenancy by the entirety – is only between husband and wife and is based upon the common law that regarded a husband and wife as a single legal person. Upon the death of either, the survivor remained as the parcel's sole owner. This form of ownership is not applicable in community property states, including Nevada.

31. Entities for ownership include:

a. Corporation – a legal entity that may own property either in severalty, if the corporation is the sole owner (without regard to how many shareholders actually own the corporation), or as tenants in common, if concurrent ownership. Shareholders are not personally liable for the corporate debts, but the corporate profits are subject to double taxation.

b. General partnership – an association of two or more persons (natural or legal) who share in the management and operation of the business. Each partner has joint and several liability for the partnership debts, but the partnership profits are not subject to double taxation.

c. Limited partnership – made up of two class of partners, general partners with unlimited liability and limited partners with liability generally limited to their investment. Limited partners cannot participate in the partnership management. Limited partnership profits are not subject to double taxation.

d. Limited liability companies – combines some of the best features of corporation, general partnerships and limited partnerships. A limited liability company provides limited personal liability exposure, full management participation and control rights and the same income tax benefits of a partnership.

e. Real estate investment trusts (REIT) – A REIT is an entity that allows passive investors to participate in large real estate projects with limited personal liability, investment liquidity and the benefit of no income taxes at the corporate level. A REIT must maintain seventy-five percent of its assets in real estate and have at least 100 owner in order to avoid paying corporate tax

f. Trusts – an entity created to own assets including real and person property for the benefit of a person. The trust is created by a trustor, who transfers ownership of the assets to the trust and names a trustee, who manages the property for the benefit of one or more beneficiaries. The three primary types of trusts are:
    1. Living trusts (also known as intervivos trusts) are created and take effect during the trustor's lifetime.
    2. Testamentary trusts are set up in a will and take effect upon the maker's death.
    3. Land trusts hold real estate as the only asset and the trustor and beneficiary are usually the same person. The ownership and beneficiaries of land trusts must be a matter of public record.

II. Land Use Controls and Regulations

The key review points for Land Use Controls and Regulations are:

Government Rights in Land

1. Ownership rights (bundle of rights) are limited by the government powers retained to protect the public health, safety and welfare. The retained government powers can be remembered by the acronym PETE for:
    a. Police power. The right of the government to enact laws for the common good.
    b. Eminent domain. The right of the government to take private property for public use without the owner's consent, after paying the owner fair compensation.
    c. Taxation. The right of the government to levy taxes against real and personal property in order to provide city, county, and state governmental services for the benefit of the people. Property taxes are levied according to the assessed value of the property (ad valorem) and the lien is superior to all other liens.
    d. Escheat. The right of the state to take property from a deceased person's estate when there is no will and no heirs can be located. An individual who dies intestate means dying without leaving a will
2. The State Enabling Acts granted the government powers to cities and counties

3. Land rights along a waterway depend on whether the waterway is navigable or non-navigable. If the waterway is navigable, the landowner owns the land to the water's edge at the high watermark. If the waterway is non-navigable, the landowner owns the land beneath the surface of the water to the center of the streambed at the low watermark.
4. Littoral rights are granted to owners of land that borders navigable lakes or oceans. These property owners have full enjoyment of the water, but they own only the land to the water's edge at the average high watermark.
5. Two primary doctrines control water use rights as follows:
    a. The riparian doctrine – common law doctrine that grants unrestricted use of the surface water to owners of land bordering the stream or river.
    b. Prior appropriation – doctrine applies to arid regions of the country and is generally translated to mean "first in time, first in use".

Public Controls Based in Police Power

6. Police power allows local communities and counties pass zoning ordinances to regulate the use and control of land. Zoning regulations are considered restrictions rather than encumbrances. Important zoning terms include:
    a. Nonconforming use – building or land used that was in existence prior to the zoning ordinance that is continued under a grandfather clause.
    b. Zoning variance – a minor change in zoning for one specific property
    c. Special use permit – allows a property owner to develop a property in the public interest, as long as it does not interfere with the intent of the existing zoning.
    d. Zoning change – may be initiated by a property owner or by the local government. The zoning change must be presented before the Planning & Zoning Commission, who then forwards its recommendation to the city council or county board of supervisors for final action.
    e. Spot zoning – a zoning change for an individual piece of property, as opposed to a change for an area.
    f. Buffer zone – a strip of land that separates one land use from another.
    g. Down zoning – occurs when a property zoned for higher-density uses is rezoned for lower-density uses.
7. Building code ordinances adopted by cities or counties regulate building construction for safety and public welfare. A building permit is required before building begins and a Certificate of Occupancy must be issued before the building can be occupied.
8. Environmental regulations and disclosures:
    a. Disclosure of the presence of known lead-based paint hazard is required of the sellers or lessors of most residential properties built before 1978.

b. The Comprehensive Environmental Response, Compensation and Liability Act of 1980 (CERCLA), also known as Superfund, was created to provide the authority and source of funding for cleaning up hazardous materials released into the environment.
c. The Superfund Amendments and Reauthorization Act of 1986 (SARA) defines who is liable to pay for the cleanup of contamination caused by past activities and created an "innocent purchaser" defense.
d. A Phase One Environmental Analysis will generally serve as an adequate defense.
e. A Brownfield is a property, the expansion, redevelopment, or reuse of which may be complicated by the presence or potential presence of a hazardous substance, pollutant, or contaminant.
f. Hazardous substance include:
    1. Asbestos
    2. Radon
    3. Lead-based paint
    4. Urea-Formaldehyde Foam Insulation (UFFI)
    5. Underground Storage Tanks (UST)
    6. Mold
    7. Electromagnetic Fields
    8. Clandestine Drug Laboratories

Private Controls

9. Deed restrictions are private limitations placed on land use. They are established at the time a subdivision is developed, or when a property owner sells the land, and are included in each deed.
10. When the deed restrictions uniformly affect all of the subdivision, they are itemized in a document called the "Uniform Declaration of Restrictions", or "Covenants, Conditions, and Restrictions (CC&Rs)," and the deed will refer only to that document.
11. A civil court action to enforce a deed restriction must be brought by a homeowner or a Homeowner's Association. If the homeowners delay action they may lose their rights to enforce the deed restrictions under the concept of Laches.

III. Valuation and Market Analysis

The key review points for Valuation and Market Analysis are:

Value

1. Value means the exchange of present worth for future benefits to the owner of the property.

2. Cost is the historical expenditure for the purchase, construction or improvement of a property. Cost has nothing to do with present value.
3. Price is the amount asked and the amount paid for property.
4. To remember the four characteristics of value use the acronym DUST for:
    a. Demand – the need or desire to possess something and having the money to fulfill the need.
    b. Utility – the capacity to satisfy human needs or desires.
    c. Scarcity – reflects the theory of supply and demand.
    d. Transferability – title that cannot be freely transferred or is restricted has little value as a purchase.
5. Types of value include:
    a. Market value – the unemotional objective price at which a seller would sell and a willing buyer would purchase, with neither party under abnormal pressure to act.
    b. Book value – represents historical cost, including capital improvements less accounting depreciation; book value is not used in appraising.
6. Economic principles of value include:
    a. Highest and best use – the most profitable use for which land can be used at the time of the appraisal; the use that will bring the greatest return.
    b. Substitution – sets the maximum value of a property by the cost of equally desirable and valuable substitute property in the same area.
    c. Conformity – a property achieves maximum value when the property reasonably conforms to the neighborhood.
    d. Balance – when a property in a given neighborhood is over- or under-developed it is not in balance.
    e. Anticipation – value created by expectation of benefits to be collected in the future or value lost by expectation of future detriments from the property.
    f. Change – a continuous process; value based on present and future changes.
    g. Competition – attracted when a business is profitable in a given area.
    h. Increasing and decreasing returns – investments to improve a property increase returns, the law of increasing return applies and value rises; additional investments do not produce a positive return, the law of decreasing return applies and value declines.
    i. Contribution – the same principle as increasing and decreasing returns, except that it applies to only a portion of the property.
    j. Regression and progression – a better property in a neighborhood of different values is adversely affected by the poorer properties (regression); poorer properties in a neighborhood of different values will increase in value (progression).

k. Integration, Equilibrium and Disintegration – the three stages of a neighborhood; development state with values increasing (integration); static period with maximum property values (equilibrium); neighborhood in decline with values decreasing (disintegration).

l. Plottage – the process of putting several parcels together as one larger parcel to achieve the highest and best use and an increase in value; also referred to as assemblage.

Methods of Estimating Value

7. The three approaches to value used by an appraiser are the:
    a. Market data approach (also known as the sales comparison approach).
    b. Cost approach.
    c. Income approach.
8. In the market data approach the appraiser considers recent comparable sales that are adjusted for difference between the comparable property and the property being appraised.
9. The cost approach, also called appraisal by summation, estimates today's cost of all improvements, minus all factors of depreciation, plus the valuation of the land using the market data approach.
10. The income approach assumes that the projected net income from the property establishes value; a capitalization of net income. The value is computed by converting the right to the future net income to the valuation amount using a capitalization rate that is the market rate of return or yield on similar investments.
11. Depreciation is a decrease in value and the three types are:
    a. Physical deterioration – the loss of value due to normal wear and tear or to postponed maintenance; can be curable (feasible to do the maintenance) or incurable (not feasible to do the maintenance).
    b. Functional obsolescence – the loss of value due to obsolete equipment or outdated architecture or floor plans; can be curable or incurable.
    c. Economic obsolescence – loss of value caused by an influence outside the property over which the property owner has no control; usually incurable.
12. Gross rent multiplier (GRM) is used as a rule of thumb for a quick estimate of value based on the relationship of comparable sales prices to comparables' monthly rental income. It is not an approach to value, but is often used as a substitute for the income approach for single-family rental units.
13. Reconciliation – the appraiser analyzes the values determined under each of the three approaches to value and uses his or her judgment in determining the best and supportable opinion of market value.

Competitive Market Analysis

14. A Competitive Market Analysis (CMA) is completed by the broker or salesperson using recent sales data on properties sold and the listing prices for comparable properties on the market.
15. The CMA is prepared to assist a seller in determining the listing price. A CMA can also assist a buyer when deciding on an offering price.
16. A CMA is not an appraisal and does not require licensure as an appraiser.

Transactions Requiring Formal Appraisal

17. An appraisal is an estimate or opinion of value as of a specified date based on analysis of factual data. The appraisal is frequently used by lenders to evaluate the value of the property being offered as security for a loan.
18. The Financial Institutions Reform, Recovery, and Enforcement Act of 1989 (FIRREA) established the requirement that all "federally related real estate appraisals" be performed by appraisers licensed or certified by the state in which the real estate is located.
19. Government-backed loans, such as FHA and VA loans, require appraisals to be completed by licensed appraisers approved by the FHA or the VA.

IV. Financing

The key review points for Financing are:

General Concepts

1. The financing of real property typically involves the use of a promissory note, along with a security instrument, such as a mortgage or deed of trust.
2. A promissory note is a promise by the maker of the note to pay a specified amount in accordance with specific terms by a certain date. The note is a negotiable instrument and can be sold by the holder of the note without permission of the payor.
3. The security instrument most often used in real estate financing is a mortgage or deed of trust. The security instruments pledge the property as security without giving up possession (hypothecation) with parties to the security document as follows:
    a. Mortgage – mortgagor is the borrower and mortgagee is the lender.
    b. Deed of Trust – trustor is the borrower, trustee is an independent party who acts for the borrower and lender and beneficiary is the lender.
4. The security instrument used, whether a mortgage or deed of trust, will contain the following provisions and clauses:
    a. Identification of the terms and conditions of appropriate repayment of the note.
    b. Legal description of the property pledged as security for the debt and a covenant of seisin that states that the mortgagor has the right to convey.
    c. Maintenance clause that charges the mortgagor with the responsibility to maintain and preserve the property.

d. Prepayment clause that enables the borrower to prepay the note prior to its due date without penalty.

e. Alienation clause, also known as a due on sale clause, that requires the borrower to obtain approval of the lender before conveyance; any conveyance of title without the lender's express approval could give the lender the right to accelerate.

f. Acceleration clause enables the lender to call the loan due and payable in the event of default.

g. Defeasance clause states that if the debt is paid by the due date, the lien that the lender holds is not valid.

h. Subordination clause in some security instruments that states that a lender in certain circumstances will agree to a lesser position of security and allow another person/lender to place a lien in front of the original lender.

5. The contract for deed, also called an agreement for sale or land contract, is a third instrument for financing a real estate purchase that combines the promise to pay and the security provisions in one document. The provisions of a contract for deed are:

   a. Includes the pledge of specific property as collateral and the terms and conditions for the loan repayment.
   b. Parties are known as the vendor (seller) and vendee (buyer).
   c. Vendee has equitable title until the total obligation is paid.
   d. Vendor has obligation to deliver legal title when the total obligation is paid.

Types of Loans

6. Interest-only loans, also referred to as straight loan, require the periodic payment of interest only. Because there is no principal reduction during the term of the loan the periodic interest payment never changes

7. Amortized loans have an installment payment of principal and interest calculated for a certain period of time. The payment remains constant throughout the life of the loan with the:

   a. Amount allocated to interest decreasing with each payment.
   b. The amount allocated to principal reduction increasing with each payment.
   c. The total payment amount is sufficient to repay the principal and interest.

8. Budget loans are amortized loans that require the borrower to pay to a trust account held by the lender a prorated amount for property taxes and insurance. This type of payment is referred to as PITI for principal, interest, taxes, and insurance.

9. Partially amortized loans calculate a periodic installment payment for a period longer than the term of the loan, resulting in a lower periodic payment for the term of the loan. A balloon payment is a note's final installment payment, which is greater than the preceding payments and pays the note in full.

10. Direct reduction loans have a constant periodic principal reduction payment plus the interest due on the unpaid balance.
11. Subprime loans are to borrowers with a credit history that indicates a greater likelihood of default. The lender generally charges higher fees and interest rates than the fees and rates charged on loans to borrowers with a better credit history.
12. Loan repayment terms include:
    a. Interest – the cost or money paid for the use of someone else's money; most real estate loans are based on simple interest paid in arrears.
    b. Usury – charging interest at a higher rate than allowed by law. In 1980 President Carter declared a moratorium on usury laws.
    c. Legal rate of interest – rate of interest that can be charged if the rate is left off of an obligation or omitted from a judgment; 10% in Nevada.
    d. Origination fee – a fee charged by a lender for the loan processing; often 1 percent of the loan amount.
    e. Point – equals 1 percent of the loan amount.
    f. Discount – charge made by lenders to increase the effective rate of interest (yield) from the stated interest rate on the note.

Sources of Loan Money

13. Real estate loan originators, who provide financing directly to qualified borrowers include:
    a. Commercial banks and mutual savings banks.
    b. Savings and loans.
    c. Life insurance companies.
    d. Pension and retirement programs.
    e. Credit unions.
    f. Mortgage bankers and mortgage brokers.
14. The secondary mortgage market is the purchasing and selling of existing mortgages and trust deeds. The primary participants in the residential secondary market are:
    a. Federal National Mortgage Association (FNMA), commonly known as Fannie Mae; loan originators sell mortgages to Fannie Mae and Fannie Mae sells mortgage-backed securities to investors in order to raise capital for the purchase of mortgage pools.
    b. Government National Mortgage Association (GNMA), commonly known as Ginnie Mae; function is to guarantee the payment of principal and interest on a pool of government insured or guaranteed mortgages by issuing a security called a pass-through certificate.
    c. Federal Home Loan Mortgage Corporation (FHLMC), commonly known as Freddie Mac; largest purchaser of conventional loans that are financed through the issuance by Freddie Mac of mortgage participation certificates, who assumes the risk of borrower default.

15. The principal residential loan programs consist of conventional loans and government-backed loans (FHA loans and VA loans).
16. A conventional loan is any loan that is not government-backed and is classified as conforming and nonconforming loans. A conventional loan that is under the maximum loan amount and meets the Freddie Mac and Fannie Mae underwriting criteria is a conforming loan. Nonconforming loans, also known as jumbo loans or high balance loans are also sold to the secondary mortgage market, but most likely to a non-governmental entity.
17. Private mortgage insurance is generally required for conventional loans with a loan to value ratio that exceeds 80 percent. Mortgage insurance protects the lender for the part of the purchase price that is not cover by the down payment and an 80 percent loan.

Government Programs

18. FHA loans - insured by the federal government; parameters of the popular Section 203(b) program include:
    a. Available to anyone who is financially qualified.
    b. Eligible properties can be from one to four units, and must be owner-occupied.
    c. A borrower is allowed to carry more debt in total than most conventional lenders.
    d. The borrower pays a mortgage insurance premium (MIP) for the insurance.
    e. Loans have no prepayment penalty and are assumable only after qualification of the new borrower.
19. VA loans – a portion of the loan is guaranteed by the Veterans Administration with the following provisions:
    a. Available to qualified veterans for the purpose of buying or refinancing real estate for personal residential use only.
    b. Maximum guaranty amount is indexed at 25 percent of the conventional conforming loan limit.
    c. No down payment loan.
    d. Interest rates negotiable.
    e. Liberal qualifying guidelines.
    f. Assumable by qualified purchaser with no change in interest rate.
    g. No prepayment penalty.
    h. Maximum loan term is 30 years.
    i. Funding fee charged for the Veterans guarantee can be paid by the veteran or the seller.

Mortgages/Deeds of Trust

20. Real estate loan classifications include the following:

a. Blanket mortgage – the mortgagor pledges more than one property to secure the note.
b. Open-end mortgage – the borrower has a pre-approved loan available for future money requirements.
c. Package mortgage – the lien is on both real and personal property.
d. Construction loan – a form of open-end mortgage that finances the cost of materials and labor for a building; the loan is a short-terms loan and must be replaced with permanent financing.
e. Purchase money mortgage –refers to any loan, whatever the source, for all or part of the purchase price for the purchase of real property; typically the term is most often used to describe a seller-carryback note.
f. Hard money loan – a mortgage given for money received; borrowing on the equity from owned property.
g. Wraparound mortgages – also referred to as an all-inclusive deed of trust; a purchase money transaction subject to, but still including, encumbrances to which it is subordinate.
h. Adjustable rate mortgage (ARM) – allows the lender to make interest rate adjustments by referring to a national index with limitations called caps on the amount and number of interest rate adjustments both annually and over the life of the loan.
i. Graduated payment mortgage (GPM) – begins with low payments but increases at intervals for a set number of years and then levels out for the balance of the term; the low payments can create negative amortization when the low monthly payment is not enough to pay the interest due.
j. Reverse annuity mortgage (RAM) – a loan based on a certain percentage of the current value that is paid to the homeowner in the form of a monthly annuity for the rest of the homeowner's life; most programs are open to homeowners who are at least 62 years of age, have ownership of their home with significant equity, and wish to use the equity in the home to cover part of their living expenses.

Financing/Credit Laws

21. The Truth in Lending Act (Regulation Z) requires lenders to reveal the total cost of loans through a standard measurement referred to as APR or annual percentage rate. The only advertising of specific credit terms without full disclosure of all credit terms is the annual percentage rate. If a borrower is pledging a principal residence already owned, the borrower must be granted a 3-day right of rescission.
22. The Equal Credit Opportunity Act (ECOA) was adopted by Congress to prevent discrimination in the loan process. A lender cannot deny an applicant credit for the following reasons:

a. Applicant's race, color, religion, sex, national origin, marital status, or age (unless the applicant is a minor and therefore does not have the capacity to contract).
b. Part of the applicant's income is derived from public assistance.
c. The applicant has in good faith exercised any right under the Federal Consumer Credit Protection Act of which the Truth in Lending Act is a part.

23. The Fair Credit Reporting Act, a federal law that requires credit reporting agencies to provide up to date accurate information. The Act also limits who has access to a person's credit history.
24. The Community Reinvestment Act was passed to help prevent redlining and discrimination by lenders. The Act is designed to ensure that banks "meet the credit needs of the community" in which they conduct their lending business.

V. Laws of Agency

The key review points for Laws of Agency are:

Law, Definition and Nature of Agency Relationship

1. Agency is usually created with an agreement but also can be implied by the agent's conduct. A fiduciary relationship exists between every principal and their agent in an agency relationship.
2. Agency relationships are consensual relationships. One person delegate's authority (the principal) and the agent consents to act.
3. An agency is a legal, fiduciary relationship where an agent works for and under the direction and control of a principal or client.
4. Agency relationships are regulated by the Law of Agency.
5. Agencies are classified as universal, general, and special.
6. The classification of agency depends on the scope of authority given to the agent by the principal.
7. Agency relationships do not require compensation, a contract or an agreement in writing.
8. The parties to an agency relationship are the agent, the principal, and the customer.

Common Types of Agency Agreements in Real Estate

9. Agency relationships include sub agency, dual agency, single agency (buyer's or sellers) unintended or implied agency and ratified an estoppel agency.
10. Dual agency exists when a broker represents a buyer and a seller at the same time; however dual agency dual agency is a common law term and Nevada Revised Statutes abrogated dual agency in Nevada.
11. The prevailing law in Nevada regarding agency duties of a licensee is statutory. The term "dual agency" is not used anywhere in the Nevada Revised Statutes titled Real Estate Brokers and Salesmen.

12. The four types of listings are as follows:
    a. Exclusive right to sell listings- listing broker receives a commission no matter who located the buyer.
    b. Exclusive agency listing-owner employs one broker as an exclusive agent, but the owner retains the right to sell the property without an obligation to pay a commission to the listing broker.
    c. Open listing- listing with an unlimited number of brokers with the commission paid to the broker who is the procuring cause.
    d. Net listing- seller is guaranteed a net amount with the listing broker receiving any portion of the purchase price over the guarantee as his or her commission.
13. A listing and an agency relationship can be terminated through completion of a sale, by agreement between agent and principal, by operation of law, and by impossibility of performance.
14. An agency coupled with an interest, such as when a broker pays on the seller's mortgage debt to avoid foreclosure, cannot be unilaterally terminated by the seller.
15. An employment agreement, known as an exclusive right to represent buyer (buyer brokerage agreement), is a contract for personal services between a buyer and broker to locate a property.
16. The buyer is the client under a buyer brokerage agreement and all fiduciary duties to the client are the same as in a listing agreement plus the duty to treat other parties (the seller) fairly.

Agency Duties

17. The relationship created between the principal (client) and the agent is a fiduciary relationship and is one of trust and confidence.
18. The fiduciary duties of the agent include these specific duties:
    a. Loyalty
    b. Obedience
    c. Disclosure
    d. Confidentiality
    e. Reasonable care and diligence
    f. Accountability

Disclosure of Agency (General)

19. A real estate brokerage and its licensee is required to disclose the type of agency relationship or representation they will have with the seller, buyer, or both the seller and buyer.
20. The agency disclosure and election should be made before discussions about a real estate transaction are held between the buyer or seller and the broker.
21. A licensee when taking a listing should review the property with the seller, complete a market analysis and assist the seller in establishing the price.

22. The agent and the principal have a responsibility to disclose in writing any material defects that might affect the consideration paid by the buyer.
23. The agent should use due diligence to search for defects in the property.

Commissions and Fees

24. The real estate broker is generally engaged by a seller through a listing agreement. Compensation to the broker is established through negotiations between the seller and the broker.
25. Setting of a commission rate for all brokerages is considered price fixing and a violation of the Sherman Anti-Trust Act.
26. Commissions are earned when the agent finds a ready willing and able buyer and mutual agreement is reached between the buyer and seller.
27. A real estate salesperson can only be paid a commission by his or her broker.

VI. Mandated Disclosures

The key review points for Mandated Disclosures are:

Property Condition Disclosure Forms

1. The seller has a responsibility to disclose in writing any material defects that might affect the consideration paid by the buyer/customer.
2. The real estate agent should use due diligence to search for defects in the property. A Residential Disclosure Guide, published by the state of Nevada Real Estate Division, aids seller in fulfilling their disclosure responsibilities.
3. The property disclosure by the seller of material facts is to be made in writing and in a timely manner and on a format prescribed by the Real Estate Division. The prescribed form 547, entitled Seller's Real Property Disclosure Form (SRPDS) is required for a residential resale, whether the land is improved or unimproved.
4. The SRPDS disclosure form must be completed by the seller only at least 10 days before the close of escrow.
5. New defects to which the seller becomes aware after the delivery of the original disclosure must be reported to the buyer before escrow closes.

Need for Inspection and Obtaining/Verifying Information

6. The real estate licensee is to deal fairly with the customer and all other parties to the transaction.
7. Dealing fairly requires that each licensee participating in a real estate transaction shall disclose to all other parties to the transaction any material and relevant facts data, or information that the licensee knows relating to the property that is the subject of the transaction.
8. The licensee is also responsible for any material and relevant facts, data, or information that should have been known if the licensee exercised reasonable care and diligence.
9. The agent should use due diligence to search for defects in the property.

10. A misrepresentation is a false statement or concealment of a material fact made to someone entitled to the information. Negligent misrepresentation is a statement contrary to fact resulting from failure to exercise reasonable care in obtaining or communicating information.
11. Fraud is a deceitful practice or material misstatement known to be false and done with intent to deceive.
12. Latent defects are hidden or dormant structural defects and if known to the seller they must be disclosed.
13. Puffing occurs when an agent makes an exaggerated statement of opinion, without intending to deceive.

Material Facts

14. The principal and the principal's agent have a duty to disclose known facts that materially affect the value of the property, which are not known to the other parties to the transaction and are not easily observable.
15. A fact is considered material if a reasonable person would attach importance to it when determining his or her course of action in the transaction at issue.
16. Under a Nevada statute, disclosure of the following information, generally considered to be material, is not required:
    a. The property is the site of a natural death, suicide, homicide, except a death that results from a condition of the property.
    b. The property is the site of any crime punishable as a felony other than a crime that involves the manufacturing of any material, compound, mixture, or preparation which contains any quantity of methamphetamine.
    c. The property is or was owned or occupied by a person exposed to HIV or diagnosed as having AIDS or any other disease that is not known to be transmitted through common occupancy of real estate.
    d. The property is located in the vicinity of a sex offender.

VII. Contracts

The key review points for Contracts are:

General Knowledge of Contract Law

1. A contract is a:
    a. Legally enforceable agreement.
    b. Between competent parties.
    c. Who agree to perform or refrain from performing certain acts.
    d. For a consideration.
2. Contracts may be classified as:
    a. Unilateral – promise for an act
    b. Bilateral – promise for a promise
    c. Expressed – verbal or written

d. Implied – created by actions
e. Executory – some action needed
f. Executed – completed contract

3. The following essentials must be fulfilled for a contract to be valid and enforceable:
    a. (C) for competent party or capacity to contract.
    b. (O) for offer, acceptance and notification, also called mutual assent or meeting of minds.
    c. (V) for valid consideration.
    d. (L) for lawful purpose.
4. The following four additional essentials are required for real estate contracts:
    a. (A) for accurate legal description.
    b. (W) for in writing; statute of frauds requires real estate contracts be written.
    c. (S) for signed by all parties.
5. The status of contracts and their legal effects are:
    a. Valid – binding and enforceable.
    b. Void – no legal effect, no contract.
    c. Voidable – one party can cancel due to fraud, duress or undue influence, but the other side cannot cancel.
    d. Unenforceable – appears valid, but cannot be enforced in court.

Offers/Counter Offers/Purchase Agreement

6. An offer is the extension of a proposal to enter into an agreement. The offeror is the person making the proposal and the offeree is the person considering the offer.
7. The proposal may be altered in writing with a counter-offer. Negotiations proceed between the parties by written proposals known as offers and counter-offers until mutual assent has been reached.
8. An offeror may rescind his offer at any time verbally until notification of acceptance by the offeree. Death of an offeror will automatically terminate an offer, whether the offeree knows of the death or not.
9. The Statute of Frauds requires that most real estate contracts be written including listings, purchase contracts and leases for more than one year. Leases of real property for one year or less are not required to be in writing.
10. A summary of document preparation requirements for a purchase contract are:
    a. Must be in writing.
    b. Must state the form of the earnest money deposit.
    c. Legal descriptions are required in the purchase contract.
    d. Documents cannot contain forged information (any changes must be initialed by both or all parties).

e. Must be approved by the broker within 5 days.

f. As soon as practical after execution, a copy must be delivered to each party signing the document.

11. The signatures on listings or purchase contracts do not need to be notarized.
12. Earnest money is a good faith deposit from the buyer to the seller providing monetary evidence of the buyer's intentions to complete the contract.
13. The earnest money deposit is not the consideration required for a valid contract and is not required for a valid contract.

Leases as Contracts

14. A leasehold is an interest in someone else's land, which allows the holder of the lease the right of possession.
15. According to the statute of frauds, a lease can be written or oral; a lease can be oral only if it is:
    a. for a period of one year or less.
    b. can be performed within 1 year.
16. A lease is a contract so the essential elements of a contract must exist. The lease must identify the property (in most cases a street address is sufficient) and must spell out the terms and conditions to ensure a "meeting of the minds".
17. The parties to a lease are known as the landlord or lessor (property owner) and the tenant or lessee, who gains the rights to possession and quiet enjoyment.
18. A real estate lease is personal property.
19. The lessor, who has given up his or her rights to possession, has reversionary rights, which means possession will be returned at the termination of the lease.
20. Leases are classified as follows:
    a. Estate for years – a lease that extends for a definite term.
    b. Periodic estates – also known as estate from period to period; a lease that does not have a definite expiration date and renews automatically at the end of each term, unless one party or the other gives notice of termination.
    c. Estate at will – created when the owner permits another to occupy a property without a formal agreement.
    d. Estate at sufferance – the lowest type of estate a person can hold; a tenant at sufferance is distinguishable from a trespasser only by the fact that a tenant at sufferance at one time had the consent of the landlord to occupy the subject property.

Rescission and Cancellation Agreements/Other Contract Terminations

21. The most common discharge of contracts is when the contract is fulfilled by complete performance of the parties to the contract.
22. The discharging of a contract without complete performance can occur as follows:
    a. Partial performance
    b. Substantial performance

c. Unable to perform
d. Operation of the law

23. Breach of contract occurs when either party defaults on the contract and can result in the following:
    a. Rescission – the legal remedy of canceling, terminating, or annulling a contract and restoring the parties to their original positions.
    b. Damages – the party who does not breach the contract can seek damages that are classified as liquidated damages, actual damages and punitive damages.
    c. Specific Performance – a judicial action to force a party to carry out the terms of the contract.
    d. Statute of Limitations – statutory law allows a specific time limit during which parties to a contract may file their legal action to enforce their rights.

VIII. Transfer of Property

The key review points for Transfer of Property are:

Title Insurance

1. A title insurance policy is an insurance contract to compensate the insured for financial loss up to the face amount of the policy when the loss results from a title defect other than any exceptions listed in the policy.
2. The three primary types of title insurance policies are:
    a. Owner's Policy – provides protection to the buyer with the face amount of the policy generally being equal to the purchase price.
    b. Lender's Policy – provides protection against defects in the title pledged as security in a mortgage or trust deed note. The lender's insurable interest is only to the extent of the outstanding loan balance at any give time.
    c. Leasehold Policy – provides protection to a tenant or a lender to the tenant against defects in the lessor's title.
3. A title insurance policy can have either standard coverage or extended coverage.
4. Standard coverage is limited to insurance against:
    a. Forged documents of incorrect marital status
    b. Documents signed by incompetent parties
    c. Unmarketable property due to defect of title
    d. An improperly delivered deed.
5. Some standard title policy exclusions include:
    a. Defects in title known to the owner
    b. Unrecorded easements, mechanic's liens, or other liens
    c. Claims or rights not of public record
    d. Rights of parties in possession (adverse possession)

   e. Encroachments or anything that could be found by survey
   f. Legal access to the property
6. Extended coverage includes all of the coverage of a standard policy, plus additional insurance against:
   a. Anything an inspection of the property might disclose
   b. Discrepancies or conflicts in boundaries
   c. Unrecorded liens, encumbrances, or leases
   d. Not having legal access.

Deeds

7. Alienation is the act of transferring real property from one person to another. The four methods of alienation are:
   a. Voluntary
   b. Involuntary
   c. By Descent
   d. By Will
8. Voluntary alienation is the transfer of ownership with the consent of the owner and includes:
   a. Selling
   b. Exchanging
   c. Gifting
   d. Dedication, which is the voluntary conveyance of private land to the public.
9. Involuntary alienation is the transfer of property ownership without the consent of the owner by operation of law. Types of involuntary alienation include:
   a. Mortgage foreclosure
   b. Escheat
   c. Adverse possession
   d. Tax sale
   e. Judgment
   f. Eminent domain
10. A deed is a written legal document by which ownership of real property is conveyed from one party to another. It is the property rights or bundle of rights that are conveyed in the deed. The parties to a deed are called:
    a. Grantor – the owner and seller
    b. Grantee – the party receiving the property ownership; buyer
11. The essentials of a valid conveyance deed are:
    a. Must be in writing, according to the Statute of Frauds
    b. Competent grantor of sound mind
    c. Definite grantee (not a fictitious person or entity)
    d. Consideration

e. Words of conveyance
f. Type of interest being conveyed (fee simple, life estate, etc.)
g. Legal description
h. Delivery and acceptance
i. Grantor's signature
j. Grantee's signature if a joint tenancy deed
k. Exceptions or reservations to title.

12. Types of deeds include the following:
    a. General Warranty Deeds – contain the greatest number of warranties (covenants) and provide the greatest protection to the grantee and impose the greatest responsibility on the grantor. The warranties are:
        1. *Covenant of Seisin* – promises that the grantor is the legal owner of the property and has the right to convey it.
        2. *Covenant of Quiet Enjoyment* – warrants that the grantee's title is good against third parties who might bring court action to establish superior rights.
        3. *Covenant Against Encumbrances* – the grantor promises that the property is free from encumbrances, except those listed in the deed.
        4. *Covenant of Warranty Forever* – the grantor promises that if title fails at any time, he or she will compensate the grantee for the loss.
        5. *Covenant of Further Assurance* – the grantor promises to obtain and deliver any instrument needed in order to make the title good.
    b. Special Warranty Deed – offers the same covenants as a warranty deed, except that the covenants are limited to the period of time the grantor was in possession of the property.
    c. Bargain and Sale Deed – provides less protection to the grantee than a general or special warranty deed. It contains only two limited warranties, namely the grantor has the right to convey the property and has not conveyed it to anyone else, and that the property is free of encumbrances, except those listed in the deed. Examples of this deed include the following:
        1. Treasurer's deed (after tax sale)
        2. Sheriff's deed (foreclosure on mortgage)
        3. Trustee's deed (foreclosure on deed of trust)
    d. Quitclaim Deed - releases or quits any claim or interest a person has in a property. It offers no warranties and is used in after-ownership situations such as in a divorce or to clear up clouds on a title. A cloud on the title is an outstanding claim or encumbrance, which, if valid, would affect or impair the owner's title.
    e. Disclaimer Deed – used when one spouse of a married couple acquires real property and wishes to hold title as separate property. The spouse

who does not have an ownership interest in the property executes and records a disclaimer deed.

Escrow or Closing

13. A chain of title shows the linkage of ownership connecting the present owner to each prior owner, all the way back to the original source of title. The chain of title can be searched by title companies or other professionals.
14. A purchaser of real estate generally requests proof that the title being conveyed by the seller is marketable title. Forms of evidence include:
    a. Abstract of title- a summary of all conveyances and legal proceedings affecting title to a parcel of real estate. It will show all liens or encumbrances affecting the property based on the abstractor's searches of county records and other official sources. Abstracts of title are seldom used in Nevada.
    b. Title insurance – considered the best evidence of marketable title, the title insurance policy requires the insurance company to compensate the insured for financial loss up to the face amount of the policy when the loss results from a title defect that existed at the time the insured received the title.
15. A closing statement is a document that accounts for the funds involved in a particular real estate transaction.
16. Each party receives a copy of the closing statement and the broker must retain a copy in the brokerage files.
17. One of two closing statement formats are generally used. The two formats are:
    a. HUD-1 statement form – used for most residential closings because the Real Estate Settlement Procedures Act require the use of this form
    b. Debit and credit statement – a type of settlement statement used for commercial transactions and residential settlements not covered by RESPA.
18. The closing statement is to be available to the buyer one business day prior to closing.
19. The purpose of the closing/settlement is:

    Signing of all documents by the buyer and seller.

    Signing of loan documents.

    Proration between buyer and seller of property taxes, insurance, rents and other expenses related to the transaction.

    Delivery of the deed and disbursement of funds to complete the transaction.
20. A real estate broker, legal counsel, or the parties to the transaction can complete the closing of a real estate transaction. Almost all real estate closings in Nevada are escrow closings.
21. The Real Estate Settlement Procedures Act (RESPA) was adopted to ensure that borrowers were provided with more abundant and timely information on the

nature and costs of the settlement process. RESPA applies to virtually all residential purchase money and refinance mortgages. Loans that are covered by RESPA must comply with the following:

a. Lender must supply the mortgagor with a special booklet titled *Settlement Costs and You.*
b. A good faith estimate of settlement costs must be supplied to the mortgagor at the time of application for the loan or within three business days.
c. The lender must use the *HUD-1statement.*
d. No one may charge any fee to the borrower or anyone else for preparation of settlement documents or any disclosures required by the Truth-in-Lending Act.
e. No one may offer and no one may accept any form of fee, kickback, or thing of value for the referral of any real estate settlement service.
f. No seller of property may require a buyer to purchase title insurance covering the property from any particular title company as a condition of the sale.
g. Undisclosed affiliations are prohibited (that is, between the broker and the mortgage company and /or the escrow company.
h. The lender is limited in the amount it can require the borrower to put into the impound account.

Tax Aspects

22. Leveraging means borrowing money from another source to supplement your own funds in completing the acquisition of a piece of property; using other peoples money.
23. The principal tax advantage for owners of investment real property is depreciation; the annual deduction allowed for recovering the taxpayer's cost of the investment property.
24. The depreciation deduction is allowable on the portion of the cost allocated to the buildings and improvements. The cost of land is not depreciable.
25. Investing in real estate provides a significant tax break, because frequently the sale of real property at a gain is taxed at the favorable capital gain rates.
26. The income tax advantage of home ownership include:
    a. Deduction of home mortgage interest expense
    b. Personal residence gain exclusion
27. The personal residence gain exclusion allows a taxpayer to exclude up to $250,000 of gain from the sale of the taxpayer's home as long as the property is owned and used as the principal residence by the taxpayer for at least 2 of the 5 years before sale. Married taxpayers filing jointly may exclude a gain up to $500,000.
28. A 1031 tax-deferred exchange is a transaction in which "like-kind" property is traded. The motivation for exchanging property is the ability to defer capital gains income tax on the transaction. Unlike property can be included in an

exchange in order to balance the equity in the trade. Unlike property received in a tax-deferred exchange is called boot.

29. A personal residence does not qualify for a 1031 tax-deferred exchange.

Special Processes (e.g. Probate, Foreclosures)(Broker Only)

30. Alienation by descent occurs when a person dies intestate which means he or she dies without a will. The property of the decedent (deceased person) is inherited by his or her heirs according to the state laws of descent.
31. Alienation by will occurs when a person dies testate meaning the decedent had executed during his or her lifetime a last will and testament. The last will and testament takes effect upon the maker's death for the purpose of distributing his or her estate according to his or her desires. The transfer of real property by will is a devise.
32. Probate is a legal process by which a court determines the assets of the estate and who will inherit the property of the deceased person.
33. Judicial foreclosure provisions are:
    a. Mortgages must use judicial foreclosure
    b. Debt is accelerated meaning that it must be paid in full; payments cannot just be brought current
    c. Foreclosure auction is referred to a Sheriff's Sale
    d. Successful bidder at the auction receives a Certificate of Sale; not a deed
    e. Owner (mortgagor) has a one year redemption period known as the Statutory Right of Redemption; the redemption period will be reduced to 30 days if the owner abandons the property.
    f. The holder of the Certificate of Sale is issued a Sheriff's Deed, after the redemption period has expired.
34. Non-judicial foreclosure provisions are:
    a. Deed of Trust can be non-judicial, but the beneficiary can elect a judicial foreclosure.
    b. Upon default, the Trustee, after receiving instructions from the beneficiary, files a Notice of Default and Intent to Sell; the intended sale cannot be scheduled for a period of at least 90 days beginning with the date of filing of the notice.
    c. A 35-day period from the Notice of Default is known as the period of reinstatement. A borrower (the trustor) may reinstate the loan by making up all back payments plus cost; the borrower is not required to pay off the entire loan balance.
    d. At the foreclosure auction, the property is sold to the highest bidder, who immediately receives title and possession; there is no statutory period of redemption.
    e. The successful bidder receives a trustee deed.

35. Lenders who take the security back due to default may still collect on the note, should the security not be sufficient to repay the debt. This is done in the form of a deficiency judgment.
36. After a foreclosure action, after all debts and costs are paid, any leftover funds belong to the defaulted borrower.

IX. Practice of Real Estate

The key review points for Practice of Real Estate are:

Fair Housing Laws

1. The Civil Rights Act of 1866 is limited to discrimination based upon race. The prohibition is not limited to housing but includes all real estate transactions. The act may be enforced only by civil suit in federal court. This law has no exemptions.
2. The Fair Housing Act of 1968 bans discrimination on the basis of race, color, religion and national origin in most types of housing transactions. "Sex" was added as a protected class in 1974.
3. In 1988, Congress added handicaps and familial status to the list of protected people.
4. The Fair Housing Act of 1968 does not apply to the sale or rental of commercial or industrial properties.
5. Important Fair Housing Act terms to know include: blockbusting, steering and redlining.
6. Under the Fair Housing Acts of 1968 and 1988 it is unlawful to refuse to (1) sell or rent housing to any person or (2) negotiate for housing, because of race, color, religion, sex, national origin, handicap or familial status.
7. Four exemptions to the Fair Housing Acts of 1968 and 1988 are provided to owners in selling or renting housing: (a) owners who do not own more than three houses, (b) owners of apartment buildings with not more than four apartments when the owner occupies one of the apartments, (c) religious organizations, as to properties used for the benefit of members only, and (d) private clubs, as to lodging used for the benefit of members only. The owners' exemptions are not available if the owner used discriminatory advertising or the services of a real estate broker.
8. Enforcement of the Fair Housing Act of 1968 was amended significantly in 1988. Enforcement procedures now include (a) administrative procedure through the Office of Equal Opportunity of HUD, which first attempts voluntary conciliation and then can refer the case to an administrative law judge, who can impose financial penalties of $11,000 to $55,000; (b) civil suit in federal court, and (c) action by the U.S. Attorney General, who may file suit in federal court and impose penalties of up to $50,000 for a first violation and an amount not to exceed $100,000 for a second and subsequent violations.
9. The Americans with Disabilities Act (ADA) provides that individuals with disabilities cannot be denied access to public transportation, any commercial

facility, or public accommodation. Barriers in existing buildings must be removed if readily achievable. New buildings must be readily accessible and usable by individuals with disabilities. Also, Title I of the ADA applies to all employers with 15 or more full-time employees and is to ensure access to equal employment opportunities for the disabled based on merit.

10. The Fair Housing Acts prohibit any advertisement of property for sale or rent that includes language indicating a preference or limitation towards a protected class.

Advertising and Misrepresentation

11. The obligation of the licensee to non-clients is to "deal fairly". A broker and his or her subagents must exercise great care to ensure that all parties to the transaction are informed and that their decision to enter into the transaction is based on facts.
12. An agent is liable for misrepresentations to the buyer/customer. An agent may also be responsible for untrue statements made by the seller that the agent then related to the buyer without confirming their truth.
13. Advertising must not include a misrepresentation of facts or misleading impressions.

Agent Supervision (Broker Only)

14. The broker shall supervise the activities of all licensees associated with the broker, the activities of the employees, and the operation of the brokerage.
15. Supervision includes, without limitation, establishing policies, rules, procedures, and systems that allow the broker to review, oversee, and manage the following:
    a. The real estate transactions performed by a licensee who is associated with him or her.
    b. Documents that may have a material effect upon the rights or obligations of a party to a real estate transaction
    c. The filing, storage, and maintenance of the documents
    d. The handling of money received on behalf of a real estate broker
    e. The advertising of any service fro which a real estate license is required
    f. The familiarization by the licensee of the requirements of federal and state law governing real estate transactions, including without limitation prohibitions against discrimination.

Ethical Issues

16. Real estate licensing is required to ensure that the public is represented by competent individuals.
17. A real estate licensee owes a duty to the public including:

    Giving equal service to all clients and customers.

    Maintaining competence in his or her field of practice.

    Refraining from the unauthorized practice of law.

Broker/Salesperson Agreements

18. Real estate licensees may associate with the real estate broker as an employee or independent contractor.
19. A written agreement between the broker and real estate licensee must be signed by both parties and dated when the licensee is retained as an independent contractor.
20. The independent contractor agreement must include material aspects of the relationship, including without limitation, the supervision by the real estate broker of the licensee's activities for which a real estate license is required.
21. The brokerage policies and rules also must be signed and dated by the broker and licensee.
22. The Tax Equity and Fiscal Responsibility Act (TEFRA) of 1982 establishes criteria to be meet for a licensee to be an independent contractor as follows:
    a. Be a licensed real estate agent.
    b. Receive substantially all income in the form of commissions from his or her designated broker only.
    c. Have a written contract giving the agent's status as an independent contractor.
23. For licensees classified as independent contractors, the designated broker can tell them what to do but not how to do it.

X .Real Estate Calculations

The key review points for Real Estate Calculations are:

General Math Concepts

1. Proper fractions are less than one whole unit. The numerator is smaller than the denominator. Improper fractions equal a whole number or more. The numerator is equal to or greater than the denominator. To add fractions, convert all of the fractions to the lowest common denominator and then add the numerators.
2. Percent means *parts per 100*. To change a percentage to a decimal, divide by 100. To change a decimal to a percentage, move the decimal point two places to the right.
3. To change a fraction to a percentage, simply reverse the process above by first converting the fraction to a decimal and then multiplying by 100, changing it to a percentage. To convert a fraction to a decimal, divide the numerator by the denominator.
4. When adding or subtracting decimals, the most important thing to remember is to line up the decimal points. Multiplying decimals is the same as multiplying whole numbers except for the correct placement of the decimal. To do this, count the number of places in the numbers to be multiplied. Then count off the same number of places in the answer and place the decimal there. If you are dividing a whole number into a decimal, put the decimal in the same place in the answer. If you are dividing by a decimal number, first change it to a whole number.
5. A rectangle is a four-sided shape whose sides are at right angles to each other. A square is a rectangle with equal sides. A triangle is a three-sided figure.

Surface Area of a Rectangle or Square = Width x Length

Surface Area of a Right Triangle = 1/2 Base (or Width) x Height (Length)

Volume = Width x Length x Depth

6. Perimeter means the "distance around" the property. To find the perimeter of a rectangular or square lot, add all four sides, or multiply each dimension by two and add the sums.
7. To calculate the area of an irregular lot, section it into rectangles and triangles, calculate each separately, and then add them together.

Property Tax Calculations

8. Property tax is calculated applying the elements to the following formula:

   Taxable Value x Level of Assessment = Assessed Value

   Assessed Value x Tax Rate = Total Property Tax.
9. Taxable Value. In 1981, the Legislature determined that a just valuation of real property should no longer be based strictly on the full cash value of the total property. Instead, the value of real property was divided into two components: full cash value of the land and replacement cost new less depreciation of the improvements, with the rate of depreciation set by statute. The resulting "taxable value" must not exceed the full cash value of the entire property. Full cash value is defined as "the most probable price which property would bring in a competitive and open market under all conditions requisite for a fair sale"
10. The level of assessment is also known as the "rate of assessment" and is generally expressed as the overall ratio of assessed value to taxable value. The Nevada Revised Statutes require that all property subject to taxation be assessed at 35 percent of its taxable value. The formula set forth in the Statutes is:

    Taxable Value x Level of Assessment = Assessed Value

    If the taxable value of a single family residence is estimated at $200,000, the assessed value would be $70,000 ($200,000 x .35 = $70,000).
11. The State of Nevada Constitution, Article 10 Section 2, limits the property tax rate to 5 cents per $1.00 of assessed value, which translates to $5.00 per $100 of assessed value. In the 1979 session, the Nevada Legislature set the property tax rate at no more than $3.64 per $100 of assess value, where it remains, plus $.02 not subject to the cap.

Lending and Mortgage Calculations

12. Most real estate loans are based on simple interest, which is rent paid only for the amount of the debt still outstanding. The formula to calculate simple interest is:

    Interest = Principal x Rate x Time

    Interest is normally paid in arrears because it accrues or is earned through the passage of time. Borrowers pay for the period of time they have used the money.
13. A **discount** is a charge made by lenders to increase the effective rate of interest (yield) from the stated interest rate on the note. The points paid for the discount are paid by the borrower at loan closing or can be deducted from the loan proceeds at funding. By actually funding less than the loan amount, the lender

increases her yield over the loan's stated interest rate. A borrower can choose from a wide variety of loan programs that offer varying interest rates and discount points.

Example: If a borrower pays 3 points for a 30-year loan of $250,000 at a stated interest rate of 6%, the actual yield to the lender is 6.287%. Because the stated interest rate does not change, the lender would fund only $242,500, keeping the difference and increasing his yield.

14. As a rule of thumb:
    a. One discount point is equal to raising the yield on a 30-year loan by 1/8 of a percent.
    b. Eight points equal a 1% change in yield.
15. **Interest rate buy-downs** are slightly different from discount points. In this case, the stated interest rate is actually reduced prior to origination. The same process occurs, but the borrower signs a note at a lower interest rate, and the lender funds the entire amount of the original principal. There are several variations, some resulting in temporary reductions in the mortgage payment for the borrower.

    Example: A home builder may have originally obtained a lender's commitment for financing the sale of the homes in her subdivision at 6.25% to 6.5%, but the market has changed. The builder may now agree to pay the 2 to 3 points to the lender to enable her to sell out her inventory at the current market rate of 6%.
16. **EXERCISE 1:** If a person borrowed $26,500 for 20 years at 15% interest per annum, using a straight note, she would pay interest of: (Select one answer from list below.)
    a. $62,200
    b. $79,500
    c. $95,400
    d. $33,300

    TELL ME WHY:

    This problem is a simple calculation of interest to be paid by the borrower. The principal amount, $26,500, will be due at the end of the note's term, in this case 20 years, so there are no installments of principal to be paid until the note is due. Therefore, the interest to be paid is calculated:

    $26,500 at 15% = $3,975 per annum (year)

    $3,975 x 20 (the term of the loan) = $79,500
17. **EXERCISE 2:** Simple interest was calculated at 8-1/2% per annum on a loan of $1,968 for 3 years, 10 months, and 20 days. The interest was **most** nearly:
    a. $589

b. $607

c. $650

d. $668

TELL ME WHY:

Again, a simple interest calculation: the annual interest on the loan, $1,968 at 8.5% is $1,968 x .085 = $167.28.

Three years interest:	$167.28 x 3 =	$501.84
10 months interest:	($167.28 / 12) x 10 =	139.40
20 days interest:	($167.28 / 365) x 20 =	9.17
Total for the period		$650.41

18. **EXERCISE 3:** If one month's interest paid on a mortgage is $200 and the principal balance is $30,000, what is the annual rate of interest?

a. 6%

b. 6.67%

c. 7.25%

d. 8%

TELL ME WHY:

In this problem, you know that the amount of interest for one month is $200 and the principal balance is $30,000; therefore, using your interest formula, R x $30,000 = $200 for one month. The annual rate is determined:

$200 x 12 = $2,400 annually

$2,400 / $30,000 = .08 or 8%

Calculations for Transactions (Prorations)

19. Proration means allocating taxes, insurance, rents, and interest at settlement to determine the amount of money to be charged or credited to the buyer or seller. In Nevada, the day of closing belongs to the buyer. In other words, beginning on the day of closing, the buyer is charged for interest, taxes, and insurance, and the buyer will receive any rent income generated by the property from that day forward.

20. There are four steps in the computation of the prorated amount:

    a. Compute the cost per day.

    b. Calculate the actual number of days to be prorated.

    c. Multiply the number of days by the cost per day.

    d. Determine whether the amount should be a debit or a credit to the buyer and seller.

21. When calculating the cost per day and the actual days to be prorated, remember the following:

    a. Use 360 days for a year.

b. Use 30 days for a month (except when prorating rents, in which case you must use the actual number of days in that month).

c. The day of closing belongs to the buyer.

22. If an item is paid by the buyer after the settlement date, there is a charge against the seller for the prorated portion of the total amount paid that represents the expense for the period from the last payment to the day before closing. The same prorated amount is a credit to the buyer, who will pay the total amount due after the settlement date.

23. If the item was paid before the settlement date and the buyer will benefit from a portion of the payment made, there is a charge against the buyer for the prorated portion of the total amount paid that represents the expense for the period from the date of closing to the end of the prepayment. The same prorated amount is a credit to the seller.

Calculations for Valuations

24. The income approach assumes that income from property establishes value. The value is computed by converting the right to the future operating income to the valuation amount using a capitalization rate**.** This approach is used primarily for apartments, commercial sites, and shopping centers.

25. Steps Involved in an Income Approach Appraisal:

    a. Estimate the annual income.

    b. Deduct the estimated vacancy rate and bad debt expense (5% is often used as a rule of thumb). The result will be the **effective annual gross income.**

    c. Deduct annual operating expenses. The result will be the **annual net income.** Do not include any mortgage payments or mortgage interest under operating expenses.

    d. Arrive at a capitalization rate. The capitalization rate is the rate of return or yield on investment. Use a comparable building's net income, divided by sales price of that building to get a capitalization rate.

    e. Use the net income divided by the capitalization rate to get the value of the subject property.

26. **EXERCISE:** A man paid $540,000 for an apartment complex that returns a monthly net income of $4,500. What is the annual rate of return of his investment?

    Step 1: Multiply monthly net income by 12 to get annual net income.

    Step 2: Divide the annual net income by the amount of the investment.

    Step 3: Convert your answer to a percentage.

27. **EXERCISE:** An apartment complex has an annual gross income of $22,800 and a total monthly expense of $900. The owner enjoys a 15% return on her investment. What is her investment?

    Step 1: Multiply monthly expense by 12 to get annual expense.

    Step 2: Subtract annual expense from annual gross to get annual net.

    Step 3: Divide the annual net by the decimal equivalent of the rate of the return.

28. Profit and Loss Problems. When dealing with a problem that involves percent of profit, you must first find the amount of profit before you can solve the problem. Then simply divide the cost into the profit to find the percent of profit.
29. Gross rent multiplier (GRM) is used as a rule of thumb for a quick estimate of value based on the relationship of comparable sales prices to the comparables' monthly rental income.
30. This formula is used for calculating the GRM:

    Step 1: Comparable sales price ÷ Comparable monthly rental income = GRM

    Step 2: Monthly rental income for the subject property x GRM = Value

    To establish the GRM for a given neighborhood, compare at least four rentals.

XI. Specialty Areas

The key review points for Specialty Areas are:

Property Management and Landlord/Tenant

1. Rent is the consideration paid under a leasehold estate. Rent can be classified as follows:
    a. Contract rent – the rental price state on the lease agreement.
    b. Economic rent –the amount that a property would bring at current market if it were not under prior contract.
2. Types of leases include:
    a. Gross lease – a lease for most residential properties that has a set rental price with the landlord paying the property charges, such as property taxes, insurance and maintenance.
    b. Net lease – used primarily for commercial properties with the tenant paying a set rent amount plus most or all of the property charges.
    c. Ground lease – a long-term lease for the use of land.
    d. Percentage lease – a commercial lease in which the tenant pays a percentage of gross income received by the tenant, in addition to rent.
    e. Sale and leaseback lease – used after a person has developed a building and wants his or her working capital available for other developments; the owner sells the building and leases it back from the new owner; the lease is normally a long-term lease.
3. The transfer of leasehold estates includes the following:
    a. Landlord/owner transfer of ownership rights- new owner takes ownership subject to the existing lease.
    b. Assignment – a tenant may freely assign his or her leasehold interest unless the lease prohibits it; original tenant has liability if assignee defaults.
    c. Novation – as it applies to a lease, make the new tenant fully responsible for the lease with no contingent liability for the original tenant.

   d. Sublease – original lessee remains fully responsible to the lessor under the original lease and becomes the sublessor, who rents to the sublessee all or a portion of the leased premises; the sublessee makes the payments to the sublessor, who in turn pays the lessor according to the original lease.

4. A property manager is a person or company who manages rental property for someone else. An investor hires a property manager to manage his or her properties and to make a profit for the investor during the holding period. Responsibilities of the property manager include:
   a. Securing tenants
   b. Collecting rents
   c. Maintaining the premises
   d. Controlling expenses in accordance with the budget
   e. Hiring and supervising employees
   f. Maintaining accounting records
   g. Making reports to the owner
5. Property management is divided in two categories: residential and commercial.
6. A property management agreement is an agreement between the owner of the property and the property manager. It establishes the rights and obligations of the parties and creates a fiduciary relationship between the broker and the property owner.
7. A broker who is engaged in property management for one or more clients must maintain two separate property management accounts distinct from any trust account that the broker may have for other real estate transactions. One trust account must be used solely for rental operating activities, and the other trust account must be used solely for security deposits.

Subdivisions

8. Except for certain divisions of land parcels, all subdivisions of land must receive approval of the county government or the municipal government if located within the boundaries of the city or town.
9. Local subdivision regulations include setting standards for streets; easements for utilities, sewers, water mains, and rights of way (including irrigation); lot sizes; setback lines; and areas reserved for schools, parks, and other recreational facilities, such as swimming pools, activity centers, golf courses, or tennis courts.
10. Sub dividers work with the local planning commission to submit a proposed subdivision for approval, which includes recording a survey, a detailed map and plat, and a detailed proposal.
11. Private land use controls are established through the recording of restrictive covenants (C.C.& R.) by the sub divider.
12. A **Developer** is defined as (1) the owner of subdivided land who, on his own behalf or through an agent or subsidiary, offers it for sale, or (2) the principal agent of an inactive owner.

13. When developers of 25 or more unimproved lots in a subdivision sell or lease to citizens of another state as part of a Common Promotional Plan, the **Interstate Land Sales Full Disclosure Act** regulates the sale or lease.
14. Unless exempt, the Act requires registration with Housing and Urban Development that should include the following disclosures:
    a. Reports on environmental factors.
    b. Assurances on the developer's commitments to provide promised improvements.
    c. The availability of utilities and sewage facilities.
    d. Audited financial statements.
15. Exemptions from the Act's registration requirements include the following:
    a. The plan offers fewer than 25 lots or lots consisting of at least 20 acres each.
    b. The lots contain an existing building on improved land, or the seller is obligated to erect such a building within two years.
    c. A professional builder purchases the lots for the purpose of constructing residential, commercial, or industrial buildings.
    d. The lot is free and clear of all liens and encumbrances at the time of the sale and the purchaser has personally inspected the property.

Commercial Property/Income Property

16. Market conditions, financing, liquidity, staying power, and the ability to control the property are all important considerations in evaluating the risk of a real estate investment.
17. Real estate investments require a long-term perspective, but there are often short-term benefits of cash flow and tax benefits.
18. Leveraging means borrowing money from another source to supplement your own funds in completing a property acquisition. Leveraging through mortgage debt increases the equity investor's rate of return, but also increases the investor's risk.
19. The principal tax advantage for owners of investment real property is depreciation. Depreciation is the annual deduction allowed for recovering the taxpayer's cost of investment property. The depreciation deduction is allowable on the portion of the cost allocated to the buildings and improvements. The cost of land is not depreciable.
20. Investing in real estate provides a significant tax break, because frequently the sale of real property at a gain is taxed at favorable capital gain rates.
21. A capital gain results from the sale of a capital asset with the net selling price exceeding the adjusted cost basis of the property.

Business Opportunities (Broker only)

22. The sale of a business often involves personal and real property. Title to personal property is transferred with a Bill of Sale.

23. The Uniform Commercial Code (UCC) governs documents and forms when personal property is used as security for a loan. A Security Agreement is the document used to create a lien on personal property and the lien is recorded by the filing of a Financing Statement, which gives constructive notice that the lien exists. A properly recorded financing statement entitles the creditor to repossess the personal property and remove it in case the borrower defaults.
24. A bulk sales affidavit is required by the Uniform Commercial Code when a bulk transfer of the business inventory takes place. The buyer of the business is to notify all creditors of the sale at least ten days prior to completing the sale. Failure of the buyer to do this can make the purchaser liable for any unpaid debts of the seller.

Nevada State Specific

I. Commission Duties and Powers

The key review points for Commission Duties and Powers are:

1. The Real Estate Commission may suspend or revoke a license for improper conduct as set forth in Chapter 645 of Nevada Revised Statutes and Administrative Code, including the following:
    a. Misrepresentation
    b. Commingling
    c. Failure to include a fixed date of expiration in a written brokerage agreement.
    d. Failure to keep a trust account or other record of funds deposited with the licensee relating to a real estate transaction.
    e. Paying a commission to an unlicensed person.
    f. Receiving compensation from anyone other than the employing broker.
    g. Gross negligence or incompetence in performing any act for which a real estate license is required.
    h. Any other conduct that constitutes deceitful, fraudulent, or dishonest dealings.

    Remember that a salesperson cannot compensate anyone, licensed or not licensed.

2. The following is the process before the Real Estate Commission can suspend, revoke, or deny the renewal of a real estate license, permit or registration:
    a. Licensee is presented by the Administrator with written notice of the charges and allows the licensee the opportunity for a hearing before the Commission.
    b. Licensee has 30 days to file a written answer to the complaint and may be represented by legal counsel.

c. Case must be heard by the Commission within 90 days of the filing of the complaint with the respondent being given at least 30 days' notice in writing of the date, time, and place of the hearing.
d. Licensee may be represented by legal counsel.
e. The case is heard and decided by the Real Estate Commission.
f. When the decision is in favor of the licensee, it is final. If desired and if legal grounds exist, the Commission's final decision that is not if favor of the licensee may be appealed by filing an action for judicial review.

3. After a hearing, any licensee who has violated any provision of Chapter 645 may be assessed an administrative fine in an amount not to exceed $10,000 for each violation.
4. A person who acts as a broker, broker-salesperson, salesperson, property manager or business broker or who advertises in a manner indicating that he or she is licensed as such, without actually being licensed is subject to prosecution before any state court.
5. Chapter 645 of the Nevada Revised Statutes authorizes the Real Estate Division of the Department of Business and Industry sets forth the duties and responsibilities of the Administrator, Real Estate Division and Real Estate Commission.
6. The Administrator is appointed by the Director of the Nevada Department of Business and Industry. The Administrator shall possess a broad knowledge of generally accepted real estate practice and be reasonably well informed on laws governing real estate agency contracts. Further, the Administrator cannot have a real estate license with or a personal and/or financial interest in a real estate firm or brokerage.
7. The Administrator heads the Real Estate Division on behalf of the Division of Business and Industry. Besides running the Real Estate Division, the Administrator also:
   a. Investigates wrongdoing in Nevada real estate.
   b. Arranges hearings for licensees with the Nevada Real Estate Commission.
   c. Arranges hearings for non-licensees before a Nevada District Attorney or the Nevada Attorney General.
   d. May issue fines from $100 to $1,000 and require nine hours of continuing education.
   e. Issue certificates for a cooperative broker.
   f. Issued registrations for owner-developers.

   Issue the year end certification of the Nevada Real Estate Education, Research and Recovery Fund.

8. The Real Estate Division administers the provisions of Chapter 645 of the Statues subject to the supervision of the Director of the Department of Business and Industry. The Division must have a principal and at least one branch office.

When the principal office is located in the southern district of Nevada one branch office must be located in the northern district of the state. If the principal office is located in the northern district, a branch office must be in the south.

9. An employee of the Division cannot have a real estate license with or a personal or financial interest in a real estate firm or brokerage.
10. The duties of the Real Estate Division include the following:
    a. Administer the provisions of Chapter 645 of the Nevada Revised Statutes and Administrative Code.
    b. Completing the day to day activities such as issuing and renewing licenses, collecting fines against licensees, and investigating real estate activities by licensees and examination of broker and owner developer office.
    c. Prepare and distribute forms for duties owed by a licensee when acting for (1) only one party to a real estate transaction, (2) more than one party to a real estate transaction, (3) a real estate broker who assigns different licensees affiliated with his or her brokerage, or (4) separate parties to a real estate transaction.
    d. Prepare a booklet concerning certain disclosures required in the sale of residential property and the Sellers Real Property Disclosure Form. The format and content of the booklet must be approved by the Nevada Real Estate Commission. Copies of the booklet and form are to be available to licensees for distribution to buyers and sellers.
11. The Real Estate Commission is composed of five members who are appointed by the governor. Members serve three-year terms with a maximum of two consecutive membership terms. If due to a resignation or other departure, the Governor appoints a replacement member and that member serves for less than 18-months that appointment will not count as a term. A term period begins on July 1 and ends on June 30th. The membership of the Commission shall consist of two commissioners each from the southern and northern districts of Nevada counties with no more than two commissioners from any one Nevada county.
12. The four requirements to be a member of the Nevada Real Estate Commission are as follows:
    a. A citizen of the United States.
    b. A resident of the state of Nevada for not less than five years.
    c. Actively engaged in business as a Nevada broker for at least 3-years proceeding appointment, or as a Nevada broker-salesperson for at least five years proceeding appointment.
    d. Take a constitutional oath of office and oath that he or she is legally qualified under the above provisions.
13. The Real Estate Commission duties are as follows:
    a. Act in an advisory capacity to the Real Estate Division.
    b. Adopt regulations establishing standards for the operation of licensees' offices and for their business conduct and ethics including provisions of the Nevada Administrative Code-Chapter 645.

   c. Conduct hearings against Nevada licensees. A Nevada licensee may appeal the decision of the Commission to an Appellate or District Court.
14. The Real Estate Division may inspect brokerage records and documents at any reasonable time.

II. Licensing

The key review points for Licensing are:

Types of Licensing and Activities Requiring a License

1. A real estate broker, broker-salesperson or salesperson is any person, partnership, limited liability company, or corporation who for another and for compensation participates in the following:
   a. Sells, exchanges, options, purchases, rents or leases, or negotiates or offers, attempts or agrees to negotiate the sale, exchange, option, purchase, rental or lease of, or lists or solicits prospective purchasers, lessees or renters of, any real estate or the improvements thereon or any modular home, used manufactured homes, used mobile homes, or other housing offered or conveyed with any interest in real estate.
   b. Engages in or offers to engage in the business of claiming, demanding, charging, receiving, collecting or contracting for the collection of an advance fee in connection with any employment undertaken to promote the sale or lease of business opportunities or real estate by advance fee listing advertising or other offerings to sell, lease, exchange or rent property.
   c. Engages in or offers to engage in the business of property management.
   d. Engages in or offers to engage in the business of business brokerage.

In addition, any person who, for another and for compensation, aids, assists, solicits or negotiates the procurement, sale, purchase, rental or lease of public lands is required to be licensed.

2. The exemptions for licensing for property management activities are as follows:
   a. Any owner or lessor of property, or any regular employee of such a person, who performs any of the acts that require a real estate license, with respect to the property in the management of or investment in the property. Management means activities that tend to preserve or increase the income from the property by preserving the physical desirability of the property or maintaining high standards of service to tenants. The term does not include sales activities.
   b. Any employee of a real estate broker while engaged in the collection of rent for or on behalf of the broker
   c. Any person performing the duties of a property manager for a property, if the person maintains an office on the property and does not engage in property management with regard to any other property.
   d. Any person engaged in property management for a common interest community.
   e. Any person performing the duties of a property manager for a property used for residential housing that is subsidized by a governmental agency.

3. The exemptions licensing for sales activities are as follows:
    a. Attorney at law in his or her normal duties.
    b. Person acting under a court order, such as a bankruptcy trustee.
    c. Trustee selling under a deed of trust.
    d. Bank or any related banking institution for property acquired for development, through foreclosure or when it is in their best interest.
    e. A corporation for its corporate property.
    f. Any person or entity when buying or selling mining claims only.
    g. Any officer or employee of a governmental agency in the conduct of the officer's or employee's official duties.
    h. Any person, who is employed by a licensed real estate broker to accept reservations on behalf of a person engaged in the business of the rental of lodging for 31 days or less, if the employee does not perform any tasks related to the sale or other transfer of an interest in real estate.
4. The following are the three types of general real estate licenses:
    a. Real estate broker
    b. Real estate broker-salesperson
    c. Real estate salesperson
5. A broker may be licensed as a sole proprietorship, but the brokerage must register with the county clerk's office and can only register one fictitious name. Alternatively, a brokerage may be licensed as a corporation, limited liability company, or partnership.
6. If the brokerage is a business entity, then the brokerage must have a designated broker who is one of the following:
    a. An officer of the corporation and the designation must be verified by the president and secretary of the corporation.
    b. A manager or member of the limited liability company and the designation must be verified by at least two members of the limited liability company.
    c. A partner of the partnership and the designation must be verified by at least two partners.
7. A real estate broker-salesperson is any person who holds a real estate broker's license, but who, as an employee or as an independent contractor, for compensation or otherwise is associated with a licensed real estate broker in the capacity of a salesperson or registered owner-developer as a sales manger.
8. A real estate salesperson is any person who, as an employee or as an independent contractor, is associated with a licensed real estate broker or registered owner-developer to do or to deal in any acts or transactions for which a real estate license is required.

Cooperative Broker Certificate (Broker Only)

9. A cooperative broker is an out-of-sate person who:
    a. Has a real estate broker license to sell real estate issued by another state.

b. Desires to cooperate with a Nevada broker to sell Nevada real estate.

10. The cooperative broker cannot be a Nevada resident.

11. The cooperative broker must pay a non-refundable fee and complete a written application that includes the following:
    a. A copy of the current license issued in the other state.
    b. A history of employment for the past 10-years.
    c. Information on the Nevada broker with whom they wish to cooperate.
    d. A history of any disciplinary, criminal or other legal proceedings involving the real estate salesman or broker-salesman who will be working for the applicant.
    e. A list of other cooperative agreements currently in effect with the Nevada broker.
    f. A photograph of the applicant.
    g. A copy of the license of the real estate salesperson or broker-salesperson who will be working for the applicant.
    h. A statement of consent to the cooperative agreement by the Nevada broker.

12. The Nevada real estate broker must verify the cooperative broker application and the Nevada Real Estate Division or Commissioners cannot assist in the application preparation.

13. A Cooperative Certificate is issued for a one-year period. During the period:
    a. The Nevada broker oversees all work performed and monies involved in the transaction under the Certificate.
    b. The cooperative broker must carry the Certificate and may authorize assistance from one of his or her licensees.
    c. Cooperative brokers are governed by the Nevada Revised Statutes and Administrative Code.

14. A client of the cooperative broker that holds a valid Certificate may collect from the Nevada Education, Research and Recovery Fund if wrongdoing occurred.

15. The cooperative broker may work with more than one Nevada broker, but the cooperative broker must obtain a Certificate for each Nevada broker with whom he or she cooperates.

Property Management Permits

16. A Property Management Permit must be obtained from the Real Estate Division before a real estate broker, a broker-salesperson or salesperson is allowed to engage in property management.

17. An applicant for a permit must complete the following:
    a. Written application.
    b. 24-hours of classroom instruction in property management.
    c. Pass the 50 question Nevada state test with a grade of 75% or better.

18. A Nevada broker who desires to offer property management services must obtain

a Property Management Permit or designate a Nevada broker-salesperson to manage the property management section. The designee must have a property management permit and must have two years of active experience conducting property management activities within the immediate past four years. A real estate salesperson with a property management permit when conducting property management activities must work for a real estate broker or designated broker-salesperson with a property management permit.

19. A property management permit is attached to the Nevada real estate license and expires at the same time as the license expires. The permit can be renewed when the real estate license is renewed and requires that three hours of property management continuing education be completed.

License Renewal, Changes in License, Terminations and Reasons for Denial

20. The status of a Nevada real estate license can be classified as follows:
    a. Current
    b. Active
    c. Inactive
    d. Inactive renewed
    e. Inactive not renewed.
21. A current license means that fees to the Nevada Real Estate Division have been paid.
22. A current license means that fees to the Nevada Real Estate Division have been paid.
23. An inactive license means that fees to the Nevada Real Estate Division have been paid, but the license has been held by the Division for 30 days or less.
24. An inactive renewed license means that fees to the Nevada Real Estate Division have been paid, but the license has been held by the Division for more than 30 days.
25. An inactive license that has not been renewed means that the Nevada licensee does not have a current Nevada real estate license. When a Nevada non-current licensee does not become current within one year, the licensee will apply as an initial applicant if he or she desire to be licensed as a real estate broker, broker-salesperson or salesperson.
26. After the initial renewal, Nevada requirements for license renewal mandate 24 hours of continuing education each two-years. The 24 hours must consist of a minimum of three hours of Contracts, three hours of Agency, three hours of Nevada Law and three hours of Ethics. Additional required topics are:
    a. For brokers and broker-salespersons, a minimum of 3 hours of Nevada broker management.
    b. For licensees with a property management permit a minimum of 3 hours of property management.
    c. For licensees with a business broker permit a minimum of 3 hours in business brokerage.
27. The education requirements to transfer from inactive status to active status vary

depending on when and how long a license has been inactive.

28. An original license as a real estate broker, broker-salesman and salesman is issued for a 12 month period. During the initial 12 month period a 30 hour post-licensing classroom course must be completed.
29. Brokers must, within 10 days, notify the Real Estate Division in writing of a change of name, business location or of a change of association of any broker-salesperson or salesman licensee.

Licensing Process and Requirements

30. Applications for a real estate broker license must be in writing, signed by the applicant and notarized. Applicants must be at least 18 years old and must be U.S. citizens or for non-citizens provide proof of the right to work in the United States.
31. The application must tell whether the applicant has ever been charged with or convicted of a criminal offense. The application must also disclose whether the applicant has ever been refused a license or had a license revoked or suspended.
32. Applicants pay an examination fee and a license fee. Applicants must also submit fingerprints and allow the Division to investigate the applicant's background prior to receiving a license.

The application must also include:

a. A certificate of completion for the required pre-licensing education.
b. Proof of a passing (75%) grade on the state licensing examination.
c. A statement the current status of any child support or if not current approval from the imposing court.
d. Occupation history for the two years preceding the application.
e. Current residence address and the residence address for the preceding three years.
f. The required fees.

33. An applicant for a Nevada real estate license cannot be a current felon, unless the felony conviction is more than three years old, or restitution was made three years ago, or the applicant has been off probation for three years, whichever of the three is the latest.
34. The Nevada Real Estate Division or Commissioners cannot assist in the completion of the application. Further, the Division can request proof of the applicant's honesty, truthfulness and good reputation.
35. The salesperson applicant must have taken 90 hours of instruction that includes 45 hours of principals and practices of real estate and 45 hours in federal and state law and ethics.

The principals and practice 45 hours consists of:

a. 21 hours of brokerage and laws of agency.
b. 12 hours of valuation and economics.
c. 12 hours of finance.

36. The 45 hours of federal and state law and ethics consists of:

a. 25 hours of ownership, transfer and use of property.
b. 18 hours of Nevada Revised Statutes.
c. 2 hours of applied practice and statutory disclosures.

37. The applicant must have passed the school examination. The applicant must also pass the Nevada state examination, which is in two parts; the national portion with 80 questions and the state specific part with 40 questions.
38. A Nevada broker- salesperson and broker must have 64 college units in the following subjects:
    a. 15 college units in real estate courses, such as real estate business, real estate finance, and real estate economics.
    b. 6 college units in Nevada law and the initial 90 hour course meet this requirement.
    c. 3 college units in Nevada broker management. This course cannot be substituted with real estate experience.
    d. 3 college units in real estate appraisal.
    e. 37 college units in any subject.
39. The Nevada Real Estate Division will grant 16 college units for every two years as a full-time real estate agent in the United States.
40. An applicant who completes the Nevada broker test before the experience and college education requirement are met can be licensed as a Nevada real estate salesperson immediately. The applicant has one year to complete the college unit education requirement and to receive a broker-salesperson license without retaking the Nevada broker test. If the college units are not obtained in one year the licensee will continue as a real estate salesperson.
41. An applicant cannot receive a real estate broker license until the real estate experience requirement has been met. The experience required to obtain a broker license is two of the previous four years full time experience in real estate. Full time means 30 hours a week for 48 weeks in a year. The experience can be completed anywhere in the United States or on a case by case basis outside the country.

Branch Offices and License Display

42. A real estate broker must obtain a license for each branch office
43. The branch office must be managed by a licensed Nevada broker or broker-salesperson who has two of the previous four years full-time experience as a real estate licensee.
44. A Nevada branch office may have a Nevada trust account and the branch manager must be a signatory on the branch trust account.
45. The branch manager has the same responsibilities obligations as the real estate broker.
46. The branch office signage requirements at the entrance are the same as the real estate broker's main office.

47. The broker's license and the licenses of all broker-salespersons and salespersons associated with the broker must be conspicuously displayed in the place of business.
48. The broker's license along with the licenses all broker-salespersons and salespersons associated with broker at that office must be conspicuously displayed at the branch office location.

III. Standards of Conduct

The key review points for Standards of Conduct are:

Advertising

1. Advertising includes, without limitation, any unsolicited printed material and any broadcast made by, radio, television or electronic means, including unsolicited electronic mail, the Internet, billboards and signs. It also includes business cards, stationery, forms and other documents used in a real estate transaction.
2. A salesperson, broker-salesperson or broker acting as an agent must not advertise property in a manner that implies that no salesperson or broker is taking part in the offer for sale, lease, or exchange. Such an ad is called a blind ad.
3. All Nevada advertisements must contain the name of the Nevada brokerage.
4. Any salesperson, broker-salesperson or broker advertising their own property for sale, lease, or exchange must disclose their status as a real estate licensee and as the property owner in the advertisement. The advertisement should disclose the status of the seller as "owner/licensee" and must not read as "owner/REALTOR". Further, the signage or advertisement should not have on the same sign or in the same ad the statement "for sale by owner" along with the name of the Nevada brokerage.
5. The designated broker supervises all advertising.
6. A licensee must ensure that all advertising contains accurate claims and representations. A salesperson or broker must not misrepresent the facts or create misleading impressions.
7. Before placing a sign giving notice that property is being offered for sale, lease, rent, or exchange, a licensee must secure the written consent of the property owner and no more than one sign can be placed in the seller's yard.
8. The name of a brokerage firm under which a real estate broker does business or which a real estate broker-salesperson or salesperson is associated must be clearly identified with prominence in any advertisement.
9. When advertising under the name of a franchise, a broker shall incorporate in a conspicuous way the real, fictitious or corporate name under which the broker is licensed to engage in business. In addition, the advertisement shall include the following statement; "Each office is independently owned and operated".
10. A licensee may use the terms "team" or "group" to advertise and promote real estate services if those terms do not constitute the unlawful use of a trade name,

is not deceptively similar to a name under which any other person is lawfully doing business and all of the following are true:

a. The team or group is composed of more than one licensee.
b. The team or group members are employed by the same broker.
c. The team or group name contains the last name of at least one of the members of the team or group.
d. The advertising otherwise complies with statutes and rules.

Property Disclosures

11. See National Test section on Mandated Disclosures for key review points on Seller's Real Property Disclosure and Disclosure of Material Facts.
12. When a unit in a planned community is resold, the seller has an obligation to make disclosures to the potential buyer.
13. The Nevada Revised Statutes require that a buyer of a unit in a common interest community be provided by the Unit owner or his or her authorized agent the following information:
    a. A copy of the bylaws and rules or regulations of the association.
    b. A copy of the declaration of covenants, conditions, and restrictions (CC&R).
    c. A statement setting forth the amount of the monthly assessment for common expenses and any unpaid assessment of any kind currently due from the selling unit's owner.
    d. A copy of the current operating budget of the association and current year-to-date financial statement for the association. The information must include a study of the adequacy of the reserves and potential for assessments for the maintenance and upkeep of the common elements.
    e. A statement of any unsatisfied judgments or pending legal actions against the association and the status of any pending legal actions relating to the common interest community of which the unit's owner has actual knowledge.
    f. The information statement required by Nevada Revised Statutes.

Preparation and Handling of Documents

14. Upon execution of any transaction document, the broker, broker-salesperson or salesperson must deliver, as soon as practical, a legible copy to each party signing the document. A salesperson or broker-salesperson must provide any paperwork to the broker with whom he or she is associated within 5-calendar days after that paperwork is executed by all parties.
15. Documents cannot contain forged information (any changes must be initialed by both or all parties).
16. Sales contracts must be in writing.
17. Listings may be oral or written, but when written the listing must contain an ending date.

18. All exclusive listings must be written, contain the Nevada Duties Owed form and cannot contain an automatic extension. The listing contract becomes enforceable when signed by the seller and a licensed agent associated with the brokerage.
19. All offers, oral or written, must be presented, regardless of price. The offers must be presented promptly and contain the Nevada Duties Owed, Nevada Confirmation of brokerage representation and the Consent to Act if the broker is acting as a dual agent. The offeree must sign and date the offer and indicate the offeree's acceptance, or refusal or rejection.
20. A closing statement is a document that accounts for the funds involved in a particular real estate transaction and it is generally prepared by the escrow agent. Each party to the transaction receives a copy of the closing statement and the broker must retain a copy in the brokerage files.

Handling of Earnest Money Deposits

21. All deposits accepted by every real estate broker or owner-developer that is retained pending consummation or termination of the transaction must be accounted for in the full amount at the time of the consummation or termination.
22. When a real estate salesman or broker-salesman associated with the broker or owner-developer receives any money on behalf of the broker or owner-developer he or she shall promptly turn over all such money to the broker or owner-developer. Promptly means by the next business day excluding holidays and weekends.
23. Unless otherwise provided in writing by all parties to a transaction, the broker must promptly deposit funds entrusted to the broker in a neutral trust account in Nevada.
24. If authorized in writing the funds can be deposited in the escrow company that is handling the transaction.
25. The real estate broker may pay to any seller or the seller's authorized agent the whole or any portion the special deposit received by the broker; however the broker will remain personally responsible and liable for the full deposit at all times.

Record Keeping

26. The following list is a summary of record retention, filing, and inspection availability requirements.
    a. A broker must keep records of each transaction for five years from termination of the transaction.
    b. All transactions must be numbered consecutively.
    c. The Division may inspect records and documents at any reasonable time.

Trust Account Management (Broker Only)

27. A Nevada real estate broker, who does not engage in property management activities, is not required to have a trust account.

28. Nevada brokers with a Property Management Permit must have two trust accounts, one for the property management operations and one for security deposits.
29. All Nevada trust accounts must:
    a. Name the brokerage as the trustee.
    b. Give the name of the bank that holds the trust account and the account number to the Nevada Real Estate Division.
    c. Allow the Real Estate Division to check the trust accounts with or without the real estate broker being present.
30. The real estate broker is required to maintain records of all money deposited into the trust account and those records are to clearly indicate the following:
    a. Date and from whom the money was received.
    b. Date the money was deposited.
    c. Dates of any withdrawals.
    d. Clearly indicate for whom the money was deposited and to whom the money belongs.
31. The real estate broker shall balance each separate trust account at least monthly. In addition, the broker shall provide to the Division on a form they provide an annual accounting that shows an annual reconciliation of each separate trust account. All trust account records and money are subject to inspection and audit by the Division and its authorized representatives.
32. Funds deposited in the broker's trust account cannot be **commingled** with the personal funds of the broker. The use of funds by the broker for other than their stated purpose is illegal and is known as **conversion.**

IV. Agency/Brokerage

The key review points for Agency/Brokerage are:

Broker/Salesperson Relationship/Broker Supervision of Licensee

1. Real estate licensees may associate with the real estate broker as an employee or independent contractor.
2. A written agreement between the broker and real estate licensee must be signed by both parties and dated when the licensee is retained as an independent contractor.
3. The independent contractor agreement must include the material aspects of the relationship, including, without limitation, the supervision by the real estate broker of the licensee's activities for which a real estate license is required. The brokerage policies and rules also must be signed and dated by the broker and licensee.
4. The broker shall supervise the activities of all licensees associated with the broker, the activities of the employees and the operation of the brokerage.
5. Supervision includes, without limitation, the establishment of policies, rules, procedures and systems that allow the broker to review, oversee and manage the following:

a. The real estate transactions performed by a licensee who is associated with him.
b. Documents that may have a material effect upon the rights or obligations of a party to a real estate transaction.
c. The filing, storage and maintenance of the documents.
d. The handling of money received on behalf of a real estate broker.
e. The advertising of any service for which a real estate license is required.
f. The familiarization by the licensee of the requirements of federal and state law governing real estate transactions, including without limitation, prohibitions against discrimination.

6. When the broker establishes the supervision system the number of licensees, employees and branch offices should be considered. A system for the monitoring of the supervision policies, rules, procedures and systems must be established and a broker-salesperson is allowed to assist in its administration. The assignment of a broker-salesperson to assist does not relinquish the overall responsibility of the broker.
7. Every real estate broker shall teach the licensees associated with the broker the fundamentals of real estate or time-sharing practice, or both, plus the ethics of the profession.
8. A broker shall not be absent from his business for 30-days or more if he is the only broker in his office unless he inactivates his license or otherwise notifies the Real Estate Division in advance.
9. Failure to observe the requirement is grounds for suspension. If a broker will be absent from his business for 30-days or more, he must designate an office manager. The designated office manager must be a real estate broker-salesperson with at least 2 years active experience within the immediately preceding 4 years or the arrangements for the designated manager must be approved by the Division.

Commissions

10. All commissions earned from a real estate transaction must be paid to the real estate brokerage and the escrow company must have the Nevada real estate broker's license number to pay the commissions.
11. A Nevada real estate brokerage that receives commissions can share that commission with the following:
    a. Licensees associated with the Nevada brokerage.
    b. Other Nevada brokerages who cooperated in the real estate transaction.
    c. Brokerages outside Nevada that have a cooperative certificate.
    d. Brokerages outside Nevada with a referral agreement.
12. Any dispute about a real estate commission between the brokerage and client is a civil matter and will not be heard by the Nevada Real Estate Commission. The dispute is between the brokerage and the client and a licensee associated with the broker cannot bring any action against the brokerage client. A Nevada brokerage doing commercial real estate can file a complaint for a legal action for commissions.

Agency Disclosures

13. A licensee is required to obtain a confirmation regarding the real estate agent relationship with the seller, buyer or both the seller and buyer. The confirmation should be documented on Form 560 entitle Confirmation Regarding Real Estate Agent Relationship.
14. The agency election and confirmation should be made before discussion about a real estate transaction is held between the buyer or seller and the licensee.
15. A real estate licensee is required to provide a Duties Owed By A Nevada Real Estate Licensee to both of the following:
    a. Each party for whom the licensee is acting as an agent in the real estate transaction.
    b. Each unrepresented party to the real estate transaction, if any.
16. The Duties Owed form is provided by the Nevada Real Estate Division.
17. Any salesperson, broker-salesperson or broker advertising their own property for sale, lease, or exchange must disclose their status as a real estate licensee and as the property owner in the advertisement and any resulting agreements.

Brokerage Agreements and Advance Fees

18. A written real estate brokerage agreement is not required for a licensee to represent a party in a transaction.
19. A written and signed agreement is required for any exclusive employment agreement. An exclusive real estate brokerage agreement must:
    a. Be written.
    b. Have a termination date.
    c. Be signed by all parties to the agreement.
20. The written agreement cannot require the client to notify the broker of the client's intentions to cancel the exclusive features at termination of the agreement.
21. The broker will not be able to collect a commission if an exclusive agreement is not in writing or does not include a required legal provision such as a termination date. Failure to meet the required legal provisions makes the brokerage agreement voidable by the client.
22. An advance fee, as defined in the Statutes, means a fee received by the real estate brokerage before the completion of the real estate transaction.
23. A licensee who charges or collects an advance fee shall within three months furnish to the client an accounting of the use of that money. The Real Estate Division may also demand an accounting from the brokerage.
24. An agreement for an advance fee must:
    a. Be in writing.
    b. Contain a definite and complete description of the services to be rendered.
    c. Specify the total amount of the fee involved and clearly state when the fee is due.

d. Not imply or purport to guarantee that the real property involved will be purchased, sold, rented leased or exchanged as a result of the services rendered.

e. Specify the date of full performance of the services contracted for.

f. Not imply or purport to represent to purchasers and prospective purchasers of the advertising or promotional services offered that a buyer for the property is immediately or soon available.

g. Provide that a full refund will be made to the customer if the services for which the advance fee is being received are not substantially or materially provided to the customer.

Duties to Client

25. The Duties Owed by a Nevada Real Estate Licensee form states the duties owed to the client as follows:

    a. Exercise reasonable skill and care.

    b. Not disclose confidential information related to a client for 1 year after the revocation or termination of the brokerage agreement.

    c. Seek a sale, purchase, option, rental or lease of real property at the price and terms stated in the brokerage agreement or at a price acceptable to the client.

    d. Present all offers made to or by the client as soon as practicable.

    e. Disclose to the client material facts of which the licensee has knowledge concerning the real estate transaction.

    f. Advise the client to obtain advice from an expert relating to matters which are beyond the expertise of the licensee.

    g. Account to the client for all money and property the licensee receives in which the client may have an interest.

26. Loyalty is the most fundamental duty that an agent owes the principal, meaning that the agent has a duty of absolute fidelity to the client's interests. There are two prongs to the duty of loyalty, as follows:

    a. The duty to disclose the licensee's interest in the transaction, if any.

    b. The prohibition against taking advantage of any situation, even if disclosed, that would harm the client's interest.

27. In offering services to the public as a real estate licensee, the licensee claims to possess the necessary skill and training to perform the employment requirements. If the principal suffers a financial loss because of the agent's failure to meet the standards of skill, the agent will be liable for the loss.

V. Special Topic

The key review points for Special Topic are:

Subdivisions and Time Share

1. The Nevada Revised Statutes (Chapter 119) provides for the licensing and regulation of any division of land into 35 or more lots, parcels, units or interests being offered for sale or lease in a common promotional plan, including

subdivisions permitted by Housing and Urban Development. This law was enacted to prevent dishonest practices in the subdividing and sale of undeveloped land.

2. The Statute requires that a **Property Report** be obtained prior to offering any of the land parcels for sale. The purpose is to ensure that purchasers receive complete and accurate disclosure of all material facts related to the subdivision.
3. A **Property Report** is defined as a report, issued by the Real Estate Administrator in accordance with Chapter 119 of the Nevada Revised Statutes, which authorizes a developer to offer to sell or sell an interest in a subdivision
4. A **Developer** is defined as (1) the owner of subdivided land who, on his own behalf or through an agent or subsidiary, offers it for sale, or (2) the principal agent of an inactive owner.
5. A **subdivision** is defined as any land or tract of land in another state, in this state or in any foreign country from which a sale is attempted, which is divided or proposed to be divided over any period into 35 or more lots, parcels, units or interest, including but not limited to undivided interests, which are offered, known, designated or advertised as a common unit by a common name or as a part of a common promotional plan of advertising and sale.
6. A **Common Promotional Plan** is defined as any offering, sale or lease of subdivided land by a developer or a group of developers acting in concert, and the land is contiguous or is known, designated or advertised as a common unit or development or by a common name.
7. Any person or broker proposing to sell any subdivision, lot or parcel in Nevada must file a **Statement of Record** with the Nevada Real Estate Division. The Administrator will examine the notice and then issue a Property Report authorizing the sale or lease of the lots, parcels, or interests.
8. A developer, who is not exempt, shall file a Nevada Statement of Record on a form furnished by the Real Estate Division.
9. Any developer who over any period divides or proposes to divide any land into 35 or more lots, parcels, units or interests must apply to the Division to register his subdivision in accordance with the Chapter 119 of the Nevada Revised Statutes and the Nevada Administrative Code, unless he is exempted from registration by the Statute and Code.
10. A developer must make a written request to the Division, specify the class of exemption for which he is applying and he must submit the information and documents set forth in each type of exemption. The following exemptions are available:
    a. The parcels are at least 40 acres in area.
    b. The property is free and clear of all liens.
    c. The construction of residential buildings by a licensed contractor who owns the land.
    d. The registration is not necessary in the public interest.
    e. The parcels are greater than 80 acres in area.

f. The disposition is to persons engaged in the business of the construction of residential, commercial or industrial buildings for disposition.

11. Before issuing a license, the Real Estate Division shall fully investigate all information included in the Statement of Record and, if in the judgment of the Division it is necessary, inspect the property which is the subject of the application.
12. After examining a subdivision, the Administrator of the Real Estate Division shall, unless there are grounds for denial, issue to the subdivider a Property Report authorizing the sale or lease, or the offer for sale or lease, in this state of the lots or parcels in the subdivision.
13. The Administrator may deny the issuance of a Property Report on any of the following grounds:
    a. Failure to comply with subdivision law or the rules of the Division.
    b. The sale or lease would constitute misrepresentation to or deceit or fraud of the purchasers or lessees.
    c. Inability to deliver title or other interest contracted for.
    d. Inability to demonstrate that adequate financial arrangements have been made for completion of all off-site improvements, community, recreational or other facilities included in the offering.
    e. Failure to show that the parcels can be used for the purpose for which they are offered.
    f. Failure to provide in the contract or other writing the use or uses for which the parcels are offered, together with any covenants or conditions relative thereto.
    g. Agreements or bylaws to provide for management or other services pertaining to common facilities in the offering which fail to comply with the regulations of the Division.
    h. Failure to demonstrate that adequate financial arrangements have been made for any guaranty or warranty included in the offering.
14. No subdivision or lot, parcel or unit in any subdivision may be sold until the Division has approved a written plan or methods proposed to be employed for the procurement of prospective purchasers, the sale to purchasers and the retention of purchasers after sale. The plan or methods must describe:
    a. The form and content of advertising to be used.
    b. The nature of the offer of gifts or other free benefits to be extended.
    c. The contracts, agreements and other papers to be used in the sale of the property.
    d. Any other reasonable details as the Division requires.

The written plan, or the methods proposed may be filed as a part of the Statement of Record application.

15. A subdivision or lot, parcel or unit in any subdivision may be sold only through a licensed broker and before any offering the name of the broker must be placed on file with the Division. Only that broker or his real estate salesman may offer or

sell the subdivided property or any interest therein. The broker and salesman, if any, shall complete the application on a form prescribed by the Division and pay the prescribed fees. Before a broker applies to become a broker of record, the broker must make a personal inspection of the subdivision.

16. A broker and a salesman may represent one or more developers only after completing an application and the payment of the prescribed fees with respect to each developer.
17. No person, except a registered representative of the developer or the broker of record and his or her salespersons, may induce, solicit or attempt to have any person attend any offer or sale of subdivision property.
18. The Property Report must be given to and reviewed with each purchaser by the broker or salesperson before the execution of any contract for the sale of any subdivision property.
19. The broker shall obtain from the purchaser a signed receipt for a copy of the Report and, if a contract is entered into, the receipt and a copy of all contracts and agreements must be kept in the broker's files within the State of Nevada for 3 years or 1 year after final payment has been made on any contract, whichever is longer. The files of the broker are subject to inspection and audit by the Division.
20. The purchaser of any subdivision or any lot, parcel or unit in any subdivision may cancel, by written notice, the contract of sale until midnight of the fifth calendar day following the date of signing of the contract. The right of cancellation may not be waived and any attempt by the developer to obtain such a waiver results in a contract, which is voidable by the purchaser. The notice of cancellation may be delivered personally to the developer or sent by certified mail to the business address of the developer. The developer shall, within 15 days after receipt of the notice of cancellation, return all payments made by the purchaser.
21. An owner-developer who is registered with the Real Estate Division may employ one or more licensed real estate salespersons to sell any single-family residence, owned by the owner-developer and not previously sold and is located in the area of the current registration.
22. The owner-developer must employ a licensed broker salesperson as the sales manager before employing any licensed real estate salespersons.
23. The Division's registration of a person as an owner-developer does not constitute licensure.
24. An owner-developer shall keep at each of the sales offices a copy of the letter of registration and shall within 10-days give written notice to the Division of any change of the name, address, or status affecting the owner-developer, or any licensed real estate broker salesperson or salesperson in his or her employ. The registration of an owner-developer will be annulled at such time as licensed real estate broker-salespersons or salespersons are no longer employed. Inactive status is not available for owner-developers.
25. A registration for an owner-developer is effective for one year after the date of issuance. An owner-developer may renew the registration by paying the required

fee and submitting the appropriate for to the Division. There is no limit on the number of annual renewals.

26. If an owner-developer fails to renew his registration, the licenses of all broker salespersons and salespersons will immediately be placed on inactive status. If the registration of an owner-developer is cancelled, suspended, or revoked, all activities pursuant to the registration shall immediately terminate and all licenses of the employees of the owner-developer shall be delivered to the Division.
27. The licensed broker salesperson acting as the sales manager for an owner-developer must comply with the following:
    a. At least 2-years of experience during the immediately preceding 4-years as a real estate broker-salesperson or salesperson licensed in Nevada or any other state.
    b. Notify the Division on the prescribed form that he or she will be acting as the sales manager for the owner-developer.
    c. Notify the Division upon termination of the association with the owner-developer.
28. A licensee associated with an owner-developer may only sell, lease, rent or offer and negotiate for the registered development of the owner-developer and the licensee cannot engage in any other activity for which a real estate license is authorized to conduct. The licensee may not be associated with a real estate broker when the licensee is employed by an owner-developer and real estate brokers working for owner-developers must change their status to real estate broker-salesperson.
29. This type of common interest community is usually at a resort or recreational area where the use of the property is desired for a short period each year. People sometimes own several time-shares at their favorite resorts in different states or countries.
30. The Nevada Revised Statutes define time-share as the right to use and occupy a unit on a recurrent periodic basis according to an arrangement allocating this right among various owners whether or not there is an additional charge to the owner for occupying the unit.
31. Each developer, through the project broker and sales agents, shall provide each prospective purchaser with a copy of the public offering statement which must contain a copy of the permit to sell time shares.
32. The Real Estate Division is authorized to issue a salesperson license that is restricted to the sale time share units. The time share sales agent may work for only one project broker.
33. The statutes also provide for the rescission of contracts or agreements for time-share and state:
    a. The purchaser of a time share may cancel, by written notice, the contract of sale until midnight of the fifth calendar day following the date of execution of the contract. The contract of sale must include a statement of this right.

Environmental Issues

34. Environmental regulations and disclosures:
    a. Disclosure of the presence of known lead-based paint hazard is required of the sellers or lessors of most residential properties built before 1978.
    b. The Comprehensive Environmental Response, Compensation and Liability Act of 1980 (CERCLA), also known as Superfund, was created to provide the authority and source of funding for cleaning up hazardous materials released into the environment.
    c. The Superfund Amendments and Reauthorization Act of 1986 (SARA) defines who is liable to pay for the cleanup of contamination caused by past activities and created an "innocent purchaser" defense.
    d. A Phase One Environmental Analysis will generally serve as an adequate defense.
    e. A Brownfield is a property, the expansion, redevelopment, or reuse of which may be complicated by the presence or potential presence of a hazardous substance, pollutant, or contaminant.
    f. Hazardous substance include:
        1. Asbestos
        2. Radon
        3. Lead-based paint-Houses built before 1978 require disclosure
        4. Urea-Formaldehyde Foam Insulation (UFFI)
        5. Underground Storage Tanks (UST)
        6. Mold
        7. Electromagnetic Fields
        8. Clandestine Drug Laboratories

Real Estate Education, Research and Recovery Fund

35. The Real Estate Education, Research and Recovery Fund (Recovery Fund) has been created as a special revenue fund for the benefit of any person (except for another licensee) aggrieved by any fraud, misrepresentation, or deceit by a licensee in a real estate transaction.
36. The fund pays only for actual, direct out-of-pocket losses arising out of the real estate transaction, in which the licensee:
    a. Performed acts that required a real estate license.
    b. Engaged in fraud, misrepresentation or deceit.
37. A person with a real estate license may not recover from the Recovery Fund for damages that are related to a transaction in which the licensee acted in his capacity as a licensee.

38. The distribution of monies from the Fund is limited to actual damages suffered up to a maximum of $25,000 per judgment.
39. The Fund will have no more responsibility to pay losses resulting from acts of one licensee once the fund has paid $100,000 in damages for multiple transactions on behalf of the licensee.
40. In order to collect from the Recovery Fund, the judgment creditor files a verified petition in the court in which the final judgment was entered. The petition requests an order from the court directing payment out of the Recovery Fund in an amount equal to the unpaid actual damages. The petition must be filed no more than 1 year after the termination of all proceedings in connection with the judgment, including reviews and appeals.
41. If the Administrator pays money from the Fund on behalf of a licensee, the license is automatically suspended. The licensee is not eligible to obtain a new license until he or she has repaid the Recovery Fund with interest at the rate of 2% over the prime rate as determined each January 1 or July 1.
42. The Real Estate Education, Research and Recovery Fund is funded by real estate licensees who are required to pay to the Recovery Fund $40 upon issuance of a new license and $40 for the renewal the license. An owner-developer is not required to pay into the Recovery Fund nor is the Fund responsible to pay on a judgment against an owner-developer.
43. If on June 30 of any year, the Recovery Fund balance exceeds $300,000, the excess must be set aside and used by the Administrator, after approval of the Commission, for education and research. The interest and income earned on the money in the Fund, after deducting any applicable charges, is credited to the Recovery Fund.

Business Brokerage (Broker Only)

44. A Business Broker Permit must be obtained from the Real Estate Division before a real estate broker, a broker-salesperson or salesperson is allowed to engage in business brokerage.
45. An applicant for a permit must complete the following:
    a. Written application.
    b. 24-hours of classroom instruction in business brokerage.
    c. Pass the 50 question Nevada state test with a grade of 75% or better.
46. A Nevada broker who desires to offer business brokerage services must obtain a Business Broker Permit or designate a Nevada broker-salesperson to manage the business brokerage section. The designee must have a business broker permit and must have two years of active experience conducting business brokerage activities within the immediate past four years.
47. A real estate salesperson with a business broker permit when conducting business brokerage activities must work for a real estate broker or designated broker-salesperson with a business broker permit.

48. A business broker permit is attached to the Nevada real estate license and expires at the same time as the license expires. The permit can be renewed when the real estate license is renewed and requires that three hours of business brokerage continuing education be completed.

Water Rights

49. In Nevada, all water, whether above or beneath the surface of the ground, belongs to the public. Water rights are subject to appropriation for beneficial use under the laws of the state.
50. The Nevada Division of Water Resources is responsible for administering and enforcing Nevada water law, which includes the adjudication and appropriation of groundwater and surface water in the state.
51. To acquire a water permit, an application must be made on an approved form and filed with the State Engineer. Once a permit is issued, the applicant may initiate the work to divert and use the water established as the beneficial use.
52. Once granted, water rights in Nevada have the standing of both real and personal property, that is, they are conveyed as an appurtenance to real property unless they are specifically excluded in the deed of conveyance.
53. Beneficial use is the basis, the measure, and the limit of the right to the use of the water. Each water permit issued is limited to the amount that can be applied to beneficial use, not to exceed a specified diversion rate and annual duty.
54. A domestic well is one well that serves one home. Domestic wells are exempt from the water right permitting process when the pumpage does not exceed a daily maximum of 1800 gallons and water cannot be furnished by an entity such as a water district or municipality.
55. An acre-foot is a volume of water equal to an area of one acre with a depth of one foot (43560 cubic feet) and equal to 325,850 gallons.
56. Potable water is water that can be safely and agreeably used to drink.
57. A water table is the natural level at which water will be located, be it above or below the surface of the ground.

REVIEW QUESTIONS

Property Ownership

1. Real estate is BEST defined as:

   a. land and the air above it
   b. land, the air above it and everything above and below the ground
   c. land, the buildings on it and anything permanently attached to the land and/or buildings and all appurtenances
   d. land an all rights in the land

2. Physical characteristics of real estate include:

   a. indestructibility
   b. scarcity
   c. improvements
   d. situs

3. All of the following are separable ownerships in land EXCEPT:

   a. surface of the land
   b. area below the surface
   c. non homogeneity
   d. air rights

4. Economic characteristics of real estate include which of the following:

   a. situs
   b. immobility
   c. indestructibility
   d. non homogeneity

5. A fee simple estate is NOT:

   a. of indefinite duration
   b. free of encumbrances
   c. transferable
   d. inheritable

6. The owner of a property with a condition subsequent has:

   a. a remainder interest
   b. a defeasible estate
   c. less than a freehold interest
   d. an estate for years

7. A life estate holder purchased the interest of the remainder man. The life tenant now holds a:

   a. fee simple estate
   b. a life estate for two lives
   c. a tenancy in common
   d. a defeasible fee estate

8. A grantor of a life estate has a:

   a. fee simple estate
   b. remainder interest
   c. reversionary interest
   d. leasehold interest

9. A fee simple estate CANNOT be owned for:

   a. a condominium
   b. property owned as tenants in common
   c. property owned as a joint tenant
   d. leasehold rights

10. Susan gives a life estate to Sally and upon the death of Sally the estate will go to Susan's grandchildren. The grandchildren's interest is:

    a. reversionary estate
    b. remainder estate
    c. fee conditional
    d. fee determinable

11. One tenant in common may NOT:

    a. use the property without paying co- tenants for the use
    b. place an easement over the property
    c. lease his or her interest without approval of other co-tenants
    d. sell his or her interest without approval of other co-tenants

12. Holding title in joint tenancy is incompatible with:

    a. right of possession
    b. survivorship
    c. probate
    d. equality of interest

13. Alan leased to Bruce for 20 years. One year later Alan died intestate leaving no heirs. The property ownership and lease status is:

a. is terminated with Alan's death
b. owned by Bruce in fee simple
c. owned by the state with the lease terminated
d. owned by the state subject to the lease

14. The unities of interest, title time and possession are required with the holding of ownership as:

a. community property with right of survivorship
b. tenancy in common
c. joint tenancy
d. community property

15. Articles of personal property owned by a tenant and solidly installed in his rented space for use in the business are known as:

a. fixtures
b. real property
c. leasehold estate
d. trade fixtures

16. An appurtenant easement on the servient tenement's property would:

a. be lost upon sale of the property
b. be included in every deed
c. go with the real property
d. be lost after one year of non-use

17. A property owner with a landlocked parcel would MOST likely ask the courts to grant a:

a. easement by prescription
b. easement in gross
c. easement by necessity
d. license

18. Mary is interested in a parcel of real estate owned by Kathy. Mary has a title report that shows the property is encumbered by several real estate financing liens. The lien with the highest priority is the lien:

a. with the lowest amount
b. with the highest amount
c. first recorded
d. with the earliest date

Land Use Controls and Regulations

19. Police power is the government's right to:

a. take private land for public use
b. enact laws for the common good
c. condemn property for the good of the public
d. tax property for cost of government services

20. The following is NOT an example of police power:

a. zoning restrictions
b. building codes
c. subdivision regulations
d. taking land for a parkway

21. Public land-use controls exist in the form of:

a. restrictive covenants
b. zoning laws
c. deed restrictions
d. assessments

22. Taking property for public use utilizing the condemnation process is under the:

a. police power of the state
b. power of eminent domain
c. power of adverse possession
d. dedication rights of the state

23. Failure to assert a right within a reasonable period may cause the court to determine that the right to assert it is lost due to:

a. laches
b. novation
c. rescission
d. reformation

24. The use of property that continues in contravention of new zoning is:

a. a variance
b. incentive zoning
c. a nonconforming use
d. illegal

25. An example of down zoning is:

a. height limitation
b. change from single family to multiple family use
c. change from multiple family to single family use
d. change to encourage redevelopment

26. A specific lien on real property includes:

a. unpaid federal taxes
b. special assessments
c. an easement
d. exclusionary zoning

27. An encumbrance on real property is NOT a:

a. homestead exemption
b. easement
c. lease
d. restrictive covenant

28. The lien that would be in first position would be:

a. an existing first mortgage recorded last year
b. current real property taxes
c. a mechanic's lien for work commenced three months ago
d. a judgment rendered and recorded yesterday

29. All of the following are methods for regulating land use EXCEPT:

a. building codes
b. zoning laws implemented by county or city government
c. deed restrictions listed in a subdivision's restrictive covenants
d. resolutions passed by a local REALTOR association

30. The following is an example of the private control of land use:

a. zoning
b. restrictive covenants
c. building codes
d. environmental controls

31. The following is NOT done under the government's police powers:

a. control the use of land
b. control rents
c. collect taxes
d. condemn as unfit for occupancy

32. Taking property for public use utilizing the condemnation process is under the:

a. police power of the state
b. power of eminent domain
c. power of adverse possession
d. dedication rights of the state

33. The process for implementing the taking of private property for public use wherein just compensation is paid to the owner is called:

a. eminent domain
b. condemnation
c. escheat
d. assessment

34. The ability of the state to enact and enforce zoning ordinances is based on:

a. police power
b. eminent domain
c. escheat
d. prescription

Valuation and Market Analysis

35. The method MOST likely to be used by a licensee when estimating the value of a single family residence would be the:

a. income approach
b. cost approach
c. market data approach
d. gross rent multiplier

36. An appraiser received figures from a CPA on past rent receipts and operating expenses. The appraiser should:

a. use the figures provided to determine the net income
b. adjust the figures provided for future occurrences
c. use the figures provided but add depreciation as an expense
d. only use the figures provided after their verification

37. An appraiser, using the cost approach to value, has the most difficulty in determining the:

a. cost new
b. cost basis
c. net income
d. accumulated depreciation

38. An amount based on historical cost and reduced by the accumulated depreciation for tax or accounting purposes is:

a. market value
b. book value
c. subjective value
d. loan value

39. In using the market data approach, the appraiser assumes:

a. anticipated future income is more important than present income
b. no two properties are identical
c. cost to reproduce now is more important than the original cost
d. risk will affect the capitalization rate

40. The function of a real estate appraiser is to:

a. set market value
b. determine market value
c. estimate market value
d. establish the price

41. A political factor influencing value would be:

a. location
b. rent control
c. inflation
d. a change in family values

42. A loss of value because of lesser value homes being built in an area would be an example of the principal of:

a. change
b. contribution
c. conformity
d. regression

43. An element that does NOT create value is:

a. demand
b. cost
c. transferability
d. utility

44. Economic life refers to:

a. age of a parcel of real property
b. period during which the building contributes value to the land
c. ability of the tenant to pay rent during his lifetime
d. depreciation of the property

45. The market data approach to value is normally used in estimating the value of:

a. an oil refinery
b. a hotel
c. a gas station
d. vacant land

46. Using all three methods of appraisal and assigning different weights to each method is known as:

a. averaging
b. reconciliation
c. bond of investment method
d. the Ellwood method

47. The market comparison method has the LEAST validity:

a. when used for commercial property
b. when there have been few sales
c. in a period of rapid change
d. when applied to raw land

48. Market value is BEST defined as:

a. assessed value less depreciation
b. the maximum price a willing informed buyer would pay to a willing informed seller
c. average sales price for similar properties in the current market
d. utility value of the property to the owner

49. In appraising a building, the appraiser would consider all of the following EXCEPT:

a. location
b. tax assessment
c. vacancy factor
d. replacement cost

50. An appraiser making an appraisal for a lender WOULD be more interested in:

a. the amount of the loan
b. the sales price and terms of the sale
c. the date and amount of a previous appraisal of the property
d. neighborhood forces outside the property itself

51. The first step in appraising unimproved property WOULD be to determine the:

a. highest and best use
b. net income
c. accrued depreciation
d. loan value

52. Functional obsolescence would NOT be caused by:

a. surplus utility
b. eccentric design
c. lack of heating and cooling
d. the proximity of a nuisance

53. The purpose of the income approach is to:

a. establish the book value
b. determine the capitalization rate
c. determine net income
d. convert net income to market value

54. The reason that the gross rent multiplier is NOT an accurate estimate of value is that it fails to consider:

a. depreciation
b. unusual expenses
c. location
d. amenity values

Financing

55. The clause in a trust deed or mortgage that permits the mortgagee to declare the entire unpaid balance due upon a default by a mortgagor or trustor is called:

a. judgment clause
b. acceleration clause
c. forfeiture clause
d. escalator clause

56. An existing first mortgage loan MAY be changed to a junior lien by:

a. a court order
b. satisfaction of the first mortgage loan
c. a subordination agreement signed by the mortgagee
d. recording another mortgage

57. A release clause in a mortgage loan agreement provides for the release of:

a. brokers from liability
b. parcels of land from blanket mortgages or trust deeds.
c. leases
d. listing agreements

58. A power of sale clause would MOST likely be found in a:

a. mortgage
b. promissory note
c. trust deed
d. listing contract

59. A defeasance clause would MOST likely be found in a:

a. mortgage or trust deed
b. promissory note
c. listing contract
d. offer to purchase

60. A mortgage that is subordinate to another mortgage, but includes the amount of the first mortgage in its balance is a:

a. blanket mortgage
b. wraparound mortgage
c. purchase money mortgage
d. open end mortgage

61. Under a land contract the seller is the:

a. vendor
b. mortgagor
c. vendee
d. mortgagor

62. Usury laws create:

a. minimum rates of interest
b. maximum rates of interest
c. length of time for repayment
d. maximum loan to values

63. When a land contract for the sale of real estate is completed by the buyer and seller, the buyer acquires:

a. purchaser's first lien position
b. equitable title to the property
c. lis pendens against the property
d. legal title to the property

64. A feature of a graduated payment mortgage is:

a. negative amortization in early years
b. lower interest rate in early years
c. constant principal payment, but variations in interest
d. an interest rate related to a sliding index

65. Equal monthly payments on an amortized loan:

a. reduce the loan principal in equal amounts
b. compound the interest paid
c. apply decreasing amounts to interest
d. apply increasing amounts to interest

66. A deed of reconveyance would be signed by the:

a. trustor
b. trustee
c. beneficiary
d. vendor

67. Truth-in-Lending disclosures would be required in an advertisement stating:

a. no down payment
b. $3,000 down
c. ten percent annual percentage rate
d. low, low down

68. A mortgage loan payable in monthly installments that are sufficient to pay the principal in full during the term of the loan is called a(n):

a. straight loan
b. purchase money mortgage
c. amortized loan
d. conventional loan

69. The advertisement of credit terms available for a house offered for sale is regulated by:

a. RESPA
b. Fannie Mae
c. Equal Credit Opportunity Act
d. Regulation Z

70. A deficiency judgment may be available to the:

a. mortgagee
b. mortgagor
c. trustee
d. trustor

71. An insurance company agreed to provide the developer financing for a shopping center at eight percent interest plus three percent of the shopping center's annual net income. This arrangement is called a(n):

a. participation loan
b. packaged loan
c. variable loan
d. open end loan

72. "Naked Legal Title" best describes the interest of the:

a. vendee under a land contract
b. trustee under a trust deed
c. beneficiary under a trust deed
d. trustor under a trust deed

73. Both FHA and VA loans cover:

a. ten-unit apartment with owner occupied unit
b. business and home loans
c. farm and business loans
d. single family and multi-family residences

Laws of Agency

74. A broker's fiduciary duty to a client includes all EXCEPT:

a. sell his property
b. care and diligence
c. loyalty
d. confidentiality

75. In a sub agency, the selling salesperson is responsible to the:

a. seller
b. buyer
c. listing broker
d. selling broker

76. A broker allowed a person to appear to act as her agent. The broker cannot deny the agency now because of:

a. ratification
b. estoppel
c. subrogation
d. reformation

77. The phrase which BEST describes the nature of a broker's duty to keep a principal fully informed is:

a. ethical conduct
b. continuing responsibility
c. fiduciary obligation
d. trustworthy business principles

78. An offer has been accepted on a 10-acre parcel, when the broker learns that the buyer has been buying up land in the area at a much higher price. The broker should:

a. notify the seller of the facts
b. recommend that the seller breach the contract
c. do nothing, as the seller is obligated to convey
d. do nothing, as agency has been terminated with the procurement of the buyer

79. A broker purchased her own listing because she knew of a purchaser who would pay more than the listing price. The broker:

a. may never purchase one of her own listings
b. has done nothing wrong if she never misrepresented the value
c. acted properly if she revealed the offer was hers
d. is liable to the seller for the profit she made

80. "Puffing" relates to exaggerations not made as representations of fact. Puffing is:

a. legal, but discouraged
b. regulated by the Nevada Administrative Code
c. illegal
d. unethical

81. In a dual agency, the broker:

a. works with only one buyer at a time
b. works with both buyer and seller
c. must work with another broker
d. works for both the buyer and seller

82. An intentional misstatement of a material fact that a party relies on to their damage is:

a. misrepresentation
b. fraud
c. puffing
d. exaggeration

83. Which of the following is NOT an agency relationship?

a. attorney-client
b. broker-seller
c. trustee-beneficiary
d. salesperson-buyer

84. In order to be able to accept compensation from both the buyer and seller a broker MUST:

a. have a listing agreement
b. have a buyer broker's agreement
c. disclose that he or she is a licensed agent
d. have written permission from both parties

85. A salesperson received 2 offers for a listed property within a 1-minute period. One offer was 2% less than the listed price and the other was 6% less than the listed price. The salesperson should present the offers to the seller as follows:

a. neither offer
b. both offers
c. highest offer
d. lowest offer

86. An instrument authorizing one person to act for another is called:

a. power of attorney
b. affidavit of title
c. estoppel
d. release deed

87. Salesman "J" shows property to buyer "T". On another day, salesman "J" tells buyer "T" that he has found a house that is perfect for him. The agency relationship would best be described as:

a. implied agency
b. expressed agency
c. general agency
d. special agency

88. An exclusive agency listing would NOT establish a(n):

a. specific agency
b. agency by implication
c. express agency
d. fiduciary relationship

89. A listing which requires the seller to pay the listing broker a commission if the property is sold is a/an:

a. exclusive agency listing
b. open listing
c. exclusive right to sell listing
d. net listing

90. A type of listing in which many brokers may be employed simultaneously is known as:

a. multiple
b. exclusive
c. open
d. exclusive right to sell

91. An owner gave an exclusive listing to broker Joe and an open listing to broker Mary. Mary sold the property and was paid a commission. The following statement is TRUE:

a. Mary must share the fee with Joe
b. Joe got nothing because he did not handle the sale
c. Joe is due a full commission
d. Joe can have a hearing with the Real Estate Commission

92. A multiple listing service deals with:

a. mostly open listings
b. only exclusive right to sell listings
c. member brokers who share information
d. owners who don't use brokers to sell

93. In order to collect a commission under an exclusive right to sell, it is not necessary for a broker to prove:

a. the listing was signed by the seller
b. the broker was the procuring cause
c. the listing was valid
d. the broker was licensed at the time

94. A broker listed a widow's property for a 7% commission. Later, the widow discovered that the broker had been listing other property at a 6%fee. Based on these fact the:

a. broker has done nothing wrong
b. broker can lose his/her license
c. widow can recover from the Recovery Fund
d. widow is entitled to a refund

95. Upon the death of a broker, his daughter, also a broker, wishes to take over his clients. She MUST:

a. inform all of the owners that she is the successor in interest to her father
b. obtain approval from the probate court
c. inform the state that she has taken over the responsibility for the listings
d. renegotiate all of the listings

96. An agent's duties to the principal include all of the following EXCEPT:

a. loyalty
b. accountability
c. obedience
d. legal advice

97. A real estate salesperson may NOT:

a. buy or sell real estate as a principal
b. accept a commission from another broker
c. show property on which his/her office has no listing
d. represent both buyer and seller in a transaction

98. Which of the following is NOT essential to the creation of an agency relationship?

a. an agreement to pay consideration
b. an agreement of the parties to the agency
c. the competency of the principal
d. a right to represent the principal

99. The relationship between the seller and a listing broker is that of:

a. seller and purchaser
b. principal and broker
c. attorney and client
d. trustor and trustee

Mandated Disclosures

100. A broker must NOT disclose to prospective buyer:

a. about structural defects
b. that zoning makes the present usage non-conforming
c. that he has seen evidence of termites
d. that the owner will accept less than the listing price

101. A real estate salesperson advised a prospective buyer that the property the buyer was considering was scheduled for annexation into the city limits. This disclosure constituted which of the following:

a. disloyalty to principal
b. misrepresentation
c. required disclosure to buyer
d. disclosure of confidential information

102. Prior to settlement, the broker discovers dry rot in the floor joists. The broker should:

a. inform the seller only
b. inform the seller and the buyer
c. refund the purchaser's deposit
d. inform no one

103. If a parcel of real estate is near a toxic waste site the agent would be obligated to:

a. conduct a phase one audit
b. do nothing, if he is not the buyer's agent
c. disclose the fact
d. disclose only if it is a superfund site.

104. Sue listed her house with a broker and told the broker that the house had termite infestation and some structural damage, but the repairs had just been completed. The broker is obligated to:

a. tell her not to tell other brokers showing the property
b. pay for all repairs himself
c. inform potential buyers
d. cancel the listing agreement

105. A broker for the seller is required to disclose to a potential buyer that:

a. the seller doesn't like the house
b. the seller is moving out of state
c. the seller is in poor health
d. a felony occurred on the property

106. During contract negotiations, a broker for the seller assures the purchaser that the property is appropriate for multi-family use. Prior to closing, the purchaser learns that zoning regulations prohibit such use. By law, this contract is:

a. voidable by either party
b. voidable at the option of the buyer
c. valid and binding on all parties
d. assigned to the broker

107. Which of the following may a broker disclose to a prospective purchaser without permission?

a. why the seller must sell now
b. why the property is not desirable
c. what the owner actually will accept
d. what the owner originally paid

108. A listing salesperson should do all of the following EXCEPT:

a. advise prospective buyers of the lowest price the seller will accept
b. verify factual information about the property provided by the seller
c. advise the seller that known property defects must be revealed to prospective buyers
d. review local zoning laws that affect the property

109. The owner tells the broker that there is a sewer on the property. A buyer purchases the property and discovers there is only a septic tank on the property. Who is liable?

a. the seller
b. the broker
c. the appraiser
d. there is no liability attaching to anyone

110. A colorless, odorless gas which is a hazard to health and is found in homes throughout the United States is:

a. asbestos
b. radon
c. urea formaldehyde
d. trichloroethylene

111. A real estate salesperson working for a listing broker must always disclose:

a. all facts to the seller only
b. all material facts to the seller only
c. all facts to both the seller and the buyer
d. all material facts to both the seller and the buyer

112. If an inspection indicates that a building contains asbestos, the results of the inspection must be disclosed to the:

a. seller only
b. buyer only
c. seller and any potential buyer
d. person requesting the inspection only

113. What form is used to provide the written disclosure by the seller of a residential property of any and all known material conditions and aspects of the property?

a. Consent to Act
b. Duties Owed
c. Seller's Real Property Disclosure Form
d. Agency Confirmation

114. The Seller's Real Property Disclosure Form must be completed by the seller at least:

a. 10 days before escrow close
b. 14 days before escrow close
c. within 10 days of contract signing
d. within 14 days of contract signing

115. A seller's failure to properly and honestly complete the Seller's Real Property disclosure Form allows a buyer all of the following, EXCEPT:

a. litigate and be entitled to treble damages
b. entitled to court and legal fees
c. have up to two years from the close of escrow to begin litigation
d. immediate recovery from the Real Estate Recovery Fund

Contracts

116. The "time of the essence" clause in a contract means:

a. offer to be presented within 24 hours
b. completion within 30 days
c. completion within the time stated
d. completed as soon as possible

117. Assuming that no written provision addresses the death of either party, a purchase contract where the seller dies after the contract is formed, but before its settlement is:

a. void
b. binding on the heirs of the seller
c. unenforceable by the sellers heirs
d. voidable by the buyer

118. The Statute of Frauds was passed to prevent:

a. bribery
b. forgery
c. perjury
d. embezzlement

119. Equitable title under an executory purchase contract refers to the:

a. seller's interest
b. buyer's interest
c. broker's interest
d. buyer's and seller's interest

120. A new contract is substituted for an existing one and the parties are relieved of responsibility is:

a. executed contract
b. rescission
c. assignment
d. novation

121. The person who signs to show acceptance of the sales contract is the:

a. offeror
b. offeree
c. grantor
d. grantee

122. A unilateral contact is enforceable against:

a. optionee
b. optionor
c. no one
d. optionor and optionee

123. Duress applied to a party to a contract makes the agreement:

a. unilateral
b. void
c. voidable
d. illegal

124. Damages for a breach of contract in excess of the actual loss suffered are known as:

a. liquidated damages
b. punitive damages
c. compensatory damages
d. specific performance

125. A contract is BEST described as a(n):

a. written agreement between competent parties to do or refrain from doing a legal act
b. offer and acceptance between parties to do a legal act
c. written offer and acceptance between parties to do or not do some legal act
d. offer and acceptance between competent parties upon consideration to do or not do some legal act

126. When a contract is ambiguous in that numbers written as words differ from the numerals the principle that applies is:

a. words take precedence over numerals
b. numerals take precedence over words
c. a void contract
d. a voidable contract

127. The offeror dies just prior to the offeree's acceptance of the offer. The contract is:

a. illegal
b. voidable
c. unenforceable
d. valid

128. The provision in a purchase contract that provides that the buyer shall forfeit the deposit if the buyer fails to complete the purchase is known as:

a. liquidated damages
b. safety clause
c. punitive damages
d. subordination clause

129. A void contract is a contract that is:

a. not capable of enforcement
b. a voidable contract
c. required to be renewed
d. in writing

130. A contract for the purchase of real estate made by a 17-year old person who intends to reside in the property is:

a. enforceable
b. voidable
c. indefeasible
d. void

131. A woman verbally agreed to a six-month lease, but prior to occupancy she changed her mind. Her verbal agreement is:

a. enforceable
b. illegal
c. unenforceable
d. voidable

132. A lessor refused to sign the lease, but accepted monthly rent from the lessee who had taken possession. The lease is:

a. a tenant on periodic tenancy
b. subject to a valid written lease
c. a tenant at sufferance
d. subject eviction without notice

133. Subordination of the right of possession BEST describes a(n):

a. hypothecation
b. trust deed
c. lease
d. exclusive right to sell listing

134. Gail leased a commercial building to Sam for ten years. After six months, Sam moved out without notice. Gail advertised for a tenant. Gail's actions most likely relate to:

a. liquidated damages
b. mitigation of damages
c. punitive damages
d. severance damages

135. Regarding a lease assignment, the:

a. assignee become primarily liable under the lease and the assignor is released
b. assignor remains primarily liable under the lease
c. assignee becomes primarily liable under the lease and the assignor retains secondary liability
d. assignee is liable only to the assignor and the assignor is liable to the lessor

Transfer of Property

136. Legal title to real estate is transferred by:

   a. delivery and acceptance of the deed
   b. recordation of the deed
   c. owner's title insurance
   d. abstract of title

137. Involuntary alienation includes all of the following EXCEPT:

   a. foreclosure sale
   b. adverse possession
   c. eminent domain
   d. dedication

138. A claim of adverse possession would not be prevented by:

   a. physically barring entry of the adverse user
   b. ousting the adverse user
   c. ordering the adverse user to desist
   d. giving the adverse user express permission to use the property

139. A deed will fail to transfer title when the grantee is identified as:

   a. "Mr. Magic", the stage name for Henry Jones
   b. Joe Smith, et ux
   c. Henry or Susan Smith
   d. Susan Smith and husband

140. With a recorded deed from the present owner of record, the one with the weakest position is:

   a. one with a prior unrecorded deed who is not is possession
   b. party in possession with a prior unrecorded deed
   c. tenant in possession with nine months left on the lease
   d. painter who is finished painting the house and has not been paid

141. "To have and to hold" MOST likely would be included in a(n):

   a. habendum clause
   b. alienation clause
   c. mortgage
   d. legal description

142. A seller who will only defend the title she is giving against others who claim an interest through or under her would give a:

a. general warranty deed
b. special warranty deed
c. bargain and sale deed
d. quitclaim deed

143. When Pete died, a signed and acknowledged, but unrecorded deed was found in his house, deeding his house to charity. His will provided that his entire estate go to his nephew. The house would MOST likely go to the:

a. charity, since acknowledgement is a presumption of delivery
b. charity, since intent was clear
c. nephew, since Pete died owning the house
d. charity, since delivery is not a requirement as to charitable gifts

144. An individual who openly, continuously, notoriously and hostilely occupies property for a specified number of years may acquire title by:

a. prescription
b. adverse possession
c. encroachment
d. foreclosure

145. An ALTA Lenders Policy is a policy for lender's protection and generally includes:

a. actual notice
b. standard coverage
c. constructive notice
d. constructive and actual notice

146. The amount of earnest money appears on closing statements as a:

a. credit to buyer
b. debit to seller
c. credit to seller
d. debit to buyer

147. The Real Estate Settlement Procedures Act applies to:

a. all mortgage loans
b. federally related mortgage loans
c. closing costs
d. interest rates

148. RESPA mandates the lender provide the borrower all of the following EXCEPT:

a. HUD booklet
b. good-faith estimate
c. estimated closing costs in three days
d. three-day right of rescission

149. Under RESPA a lender is required to provide a borrower a:

a. three-day right to rescind
b. property advertising material
c. good faith estimate and HUD book
d. annual percentage rate

150. To be valid, a deed requires:

a. recording
b. signature of grantee
c. a legal street address
d. delivery and acceptance

151. A valid deed does NOT require a:

a. signature of the grantee
b. statement of consideration
c. legal description of the property
d. grantor with legal capacity

152. Mary, a single individual, may exclude up to $250,000 of capital gain on the sale of her residence if:

a. she owned it for one year
b. the residence was her principal residence for two of the preceding five years
c. she does not have a second residence as a vacation home
d. she has not sold a residence within the past five years

153. A commercial property was purchased for $185,000 and has been depreciated to a $61,000 book value. When the property sold for $163,000, there is a:

a. $22,000 taxable loss
b. $102,000 taxable gain
c. $39,000 taxable gain
d. $124,000 taxable gain

154. The statutory redemption period after a trustee's sale is:

a. 90 days
b. 6 months
c. one year
d. none

Practice of Real Estate

155. It is illegal for a real estate salesperson to:

a. explain the legal transfer of title to a client
b. advise a client to hold title to a property in severalty
c. advise a client to get a home inspection
d. tell a client to consult an attorney

156. In the absence of a prior agreement defining when the broker's commission is earned, commission is "earned" when:

a. the deal is consummated
b. buyer and seller have a meeting of the minds
c. the broker introduces a buyer to the seller
d. the deed is delivered

157. Salespeople may be compensated for their services by:

a. any broker
b. another salesperson
c. the owner
d. his or her broker

158. A salesperson accepts a postdated check as earnest money. The seller accepts the buyers offer, without any knowledge of the postdated check. What may the seller do if the check "bounces"?

a. nothing because his/her salesperson knew the check was postdated
b. bring action to recover from the broker
c. recover directly from the recovery fund
d. hold the salesperson responsible

159. A client refuses to sell his property when presented with an offer according to terms of a valid listing. The client:

a. does not have to sell
b. may be sued for specific performance
c. can be sued for damages by buyer
d. can be sued by the salesperson

160. The holder of a general power of attorney, in dealing with real property of his or her principal, could NOT:

a. buy it
b. sell it
c. lease it
d. give an exclusive right to sell listing

161. What is the practice of encouraging the sale of properties in a particular neighborhood by revealing that members of a protected class are entering the neighborhood?

a. blockbusting
b. redlining
c. market hysteria
d. panic-selling

162. What does the Civil Rights Act of 1866 prohibit?

a. steering
b. blockbusting
c. discrimination based on race
d. discrimination against handicapped persons

163. A developer in selling homes would be advertising illegally if he advertised:

a. for "singles only"
b. to persons of a specific national origin
c. for persons with a "poor credit history"
d. to persons of a specific political party

164. A woman's rights group established a non-profit housing project with preference to single women with children. Their action is:

a. proper if the organization is also non-profit
b. proper if there is no racial discrimination
c. improper under the Civil Rights Act of 1866
d. improper under the Civil Rights Act of 1968

165. The Sherman Antitrust Act prohibits brokers from:

a. advertising down payment amounts
b. discriminating on the basis of race, religion or national origin
c. setting standard commission rates
d. selling each other's listings

166. A broker's obligation to the parties in a real estate transaction other than his or her client includes:

a. there are no obligations to non-clients
b. the same as to the principal
c. loyalty
d. dealing fairly

167. Commingling is the opposite of:

a. subrogation
b. substitution
c. subordination
d. separation

168. An agent takes a buyer to a specific neighborhood based on their ethnicity. This is an example of:

a. blockbusting
b. redlining
c. steering
d. hypothecation

169. A lawsuit by a principal against a broker who failed to follow instructions will probably result in:

a. loss of broker's license
b. fine and/or jail time
c. money damages
d. a judgment in favor of the broker

170. A broker, in dealing with the public may NOT:

a. keep silent about a material fact in the transaction
b. take an option
c. accept a commission from both buyer and seller
d. negotiate different commission rates with different owners

171. Conversion would occur when a licensee:

a. uses client funds to pay brokerage rent
b. engages in blockbusting
c. fails to indicate an agency relationship
d. uses unlicensed people to solicit business

172. What would be violated if a seller required that title insurance be obtained from a particular provider?

a. code of ethics
b. Fair Housing Act
c. Equal Credit Opportunity Act
d. Real Estate Settlement Procedures Act

173. A salesperson has acted in an unethical manner. His/her broker:

a. may be liable for a failure to supervise
b. would not be liable
c. should ignore the problem
d. should immediately terminate the salesperson

174. A broker sold an apartment building to a syndicate of which the broker was a member without informing the seller of his interest. Before closing, the owner discovered the broker's interest and refused to sell. The results of a lawsuit by the broker to collect the commission would most likely be:

a. revocation of the broker's license
b. payment of a commission to the broker
c. release of the owner's obligation to pay a commission
d. an order for specific performance on behalf of the buyer

175. The real estate broker's equivalent of medical doctor's malpractice insurance is:

a. extended homeowner's coverage
b. errors and omissions insurance
c. realty malpractice insurance
d. irate homeowner insurance

176. If , upon receiving an offer to purchase under certain terms and conditions, the seller makes a conditional acceptance, the offeror is:

a. bound by the original offer
b. bound to accept the counter offer
c. relieved from the original offer at the seller's option
d. relieved from the original offer unconditionally

177. The termination of an offer would NOT be caused by:

a. request by the offeree for more time for acceptance
b. revocation by the offeror
c. acceptance contingent upon a change in price
d. death of the offeror

178. An offer to purchase states that it would be kept open for acceptance for three days. The day after making the offer, and before acceptance, it is withdrawn. The real estate agent should inform the offeror that:

a. he may withdraw without penalty
b. it will mean the forfeiture of earnest money
c. only death can revoke the offer
d. an offer is irrevocable

Real Estate Calculations

179. A duplex whose total rent is $1,250 per month, is in an area of a smaller duplex in similar condition that rents for $440 per unit and just sold for $132,000. Using this information, the larger duplex would have a value of:

a. $150,000
b. $167,500
c. $187,500
d. $192,500

180. A property has a net income of $30,000. an appraiser decides to use a 12 percent capitalization rate rather than a ten percent rate. This will result in a:

a. two percent increase in value
b. $50,000 increase in appraised value
c. $50,000 decrease in appraised value
d. two percent decrease in appraised value

181. A savings and loan making an 80% loan-to-value on a triplex for $420,000 would make a loan of:

a. $294,000
b. $336,000
c. $399,000
d. $371,200

182. On February 1, a mortgagor makes a $638 monthly payment on her mortgage, which has an interest rate of 10%. The mortgagee allocates $500 to the payment of interest. What is the principal balance due on the mortgage on February 2?

a. $60,000
b. $59,862
c. $63,662
d. $63,850

183. A $45,000 straight loan at 7% interest was repaid in six months. The total amount repaid was:

a. $3,150
b. $1,575
c. $46,575
d. $48,150

184. A buyer assumed a seller's existing 7%, $180,000 first deed of trust on the settlement date of June 13. The seller made the monthly payment of June 1 with interest in arrears. The correct settlement statement entry for the interest is:

a. $630 seller's credit
b. $420 buyer's debit
c. $630 seller's debit
d. $420 seller's debit

185. A five-acre rectangular parcel is divided into six equal lots, each having a depth of 250'. The width of each lot is approximately:

a. 145.2'
b. 174.24'
c. 208.7'
d. 871.2'

186. The W1/2 of the NW1/4 of the NW1/4 of the SE1/4 of the SW1/4 of a section is to be paved for parking at a cost of $1.20 per square foot. The total paving cost will be:

a. $16,336
b. $32,668
c. $65,340
d. $130,677

187. The S1/2 of NW1/4 of SE1/4 of NW1/4 of a section contains:

a. 1 ¼ acres
b. 2 ½ acres
c. 5 acres
d. 10 acres

188. A buyer, purchasing a home, assumes the seller's loan balance of $93,000 with 7.5% interest in arrears. If the September 1 payment has been made and the closing is scheduled for September 20, the buyer is entitled to a credit for interest at the closing of:

a. $388
b. $368
c. $213
d. $581

189. A transaction involving a commercial office building will close on June 13th. The building has 24 leases with total annual rentals of $2,256,000. Monthly rentals are current as of June 1st. Security deposits total $1,804,800. The leases begin to expire in August; all of them must be rewritten by October 1st. At closing the seller will be charged for rents collected and security deposits a total of:

a. $1,880,000
b. $1,917,600
c. $1,992,800
d. $2,068,000

190. A seller is willing to pay 2 discount points for the borrower, who is obtaining an 80% loan to value. The house was listed at $127,000, even though it was appraised at $117,000, and the assessed value is $111,000. The buyer has contracted to pay $125,000, but the seller has agreed to pay discount points of:

a. $2,540
b. $2000
c. $1,872
d. $1,776

191. An owner lists a lot for sale with a broker to net $70,500 after paying the broker a 7% commission. At what price would the broker have to sell the property to receive a 7% commission?

a. $75,435
b. $75,806
c. $77,585
d. $72,125

Specialty Areas

192. A property manager may NOT receive:

a. reimbursement for out of pocket expenses
b. free rent on an apartment unit
c. monthly management fees
d. rebates from suppliers

193. What BEST describes chattel?

a. a fixture
b. personal property
c. personal property that has been converted to real estate
d. a mortgage on personal property

194. Carl leases a building and installs shelves, cabinets, refrigerator and other articles for use in the business. When the lease expires:

a. Carl can remove the equipment installed before his lease expires
b. Carl must leave them for the landlord's benefit
c. Carl can remove them ant any time after expiration
d. Landlord must pay Carl for any articles left.

195. What is NOT part of the property manager's responsibilities?

a. ethics
b. keeping up with rental rates in the area
c. telling the owner the market value of the building
d. keeping current with vacancies

196. What is not part of a typical property management agreement?

a. beginning and ending date
b. frequency of management reports
c. cancellation clause
d. annual budget

197. Which of the following would NOT be part of the landlord tenant act:

a. security deposits regulations
b. property management agreement regulations
c. notices for eviction
d. notice of intent to enter

198. A landlord wishes to show a party your apartment. He may do so with which of the following notices:

a. 24 hours
b. 48 hours
c. 72 hours
d. 96 hours

199. All of the following are required of property managers EXCEPT:

a. showing and leasing property
b. determining the owner's objectives
c. collecting rent
d. providing security for the tenants

200. An owner of a condominium apartment holds:

a. a fee simple title
b. a leasehold interest
c. title the same as a cooperative apartment
d. a life estate

Nevada State Specific-Commission Duties and Powers

201. The Real Estate Commission consists of:

a. 5 members
b. 6 members
c. 7 members
d. 8 members

202. The Real Estate Commission is required to do all of the following EXCEPT:

a. manage the Real Estate Division
b. act as advisor to the Real Estate Division
c. adopt regulations
d. conduct administrative hearings

203. The term of office for a member of the Nevada Real Estate Commission is:

a. 6 years
b. 4 years
c. 3 years
d. 2 years

204. When the Administrator receives a written complaint against a licensee, the Administrator will:

a. automatically suspend the license
b. revoke the license
c. turn the matter over to civil court
d. allow an opportunity for a hearing before the Real Estate Commission.

205. A Nevada Real Estate Commissioner is:

a. appointed by the state legislature
b. appointed by the Governor
c. elected by popular vote
d. appointed by the Secretary of State

206. Engaging in the sale of real estate when a license is required but in fact acting without a license is:

a. a misdemeanor
b. not subject to action by the Real Estate Division because the party is not licensed
c. subject to prosecution before any state court
d. subject to action before the Real Estate Commission

207. The Real Estate Division is managed by the:

a. Real Estate Commission
b. Administrator
c. state legislature
d. Commissioner

208. The head of the Nevada Real Estate division is appointed by the:

a. Director of the Nevada Department of Business and Industry
b. Real Estate Commission
c. Governor in Nevada
d. State Legislature

209. After a hearing before the Real Estate Commission, any licensee who has violated Chapter 645 of the NRS may be assessed an administrative fine in an amount not to exceed:

a. $,1000 per violation
b. $5,000 per violation
c. $10,000 per violation
d. $10,000 in total

Nevada State Specific-Licensing

210. When a license is issued to a corporation, the designated broker must be:

a. the corporation president
b. one officer of the corporation
c. all officers of the corporation
d. the sales manager of the corporation

211. The primary purpose of the real estate licensing statute is to:

a. have trained professionals
b. protect brokers against incompetent salespeople
c. avoid cutthroat competition
d. protect the public

212. The individual that is required to have a real estate license is a(n):

a. developer selling more than ten homes
b. attorney in fact selling property for a principal
c. trustee selling under a court order
d. attorney at law taking a listing

213. If a real estate salesperson license is not renewed its is:

a. automatically reinstated for 30 days
b. automatically reinstated for 6 months
c. automatically reinstated for one year
d. a non-current license

214. In Nevada, the person who is exempt from the real estate licensing law is a:

a. person who sells subdivision lots
b. trustee in bankruptcy
c. person handling leases only
d. person selling custom built homes

215. If a broker loses his or her license, the salespeople can:

a. close all transactions as soon as possible
b. activate their licenses with another broker
c. wait to see if their broker gets his license reinstated
d. continue to operate as before

216. When a salesperson with a brokers license is employed by a broker, the salesperson has a:

a. salesperson license
b. broker-salesperson license
c. broker license
d. cooperative broker permit

217. In Nevada, the qualification that is NOT required to obtain a real estate salesperson license is:

a. 90 hours of education
b. 90 days of residence
c. passing the state examination
d. minimum age

218. A broker for a subdivision employs hostesses to show model homes and spec houses. They only show features and give pricing information. The hostesses:

a. do not need a license because they are employed by a licensed broker
b. do not need a license because they do not negotiate contract terms
c. must be licensed
d. do not need a license if they do not accept deposits

219. A real estate salesperson license that has paid the required fees to the Real Estate Division, but the license is held by the Division for 45 days is classified as:

a. active
b. inactive
c. inactive-renewed
d. inactive-not renewed

220. During the initial 12-month licensing period, the licensee must complete a:

a. 24-hours of continuing education
b. 30-hour post licensing classroom course
c. 30 hours of continuing education
d. 12 hours of continuing education

221. An applicant for a Property Management Permit must complete all of the following EXCEPT:

a. written application
b. 24 hours of classroom instruction in property management
c. pass the 50-question Nevada test with a grade of 75% or better
d. supply fingerprints

222. A real estate brokerage branch office:

a. must have signage similar to the main office
b. does not need a separate license
c. can have a licensed salesperson as the manager
d. may not have a Nevada trust account

223. After the initial 12 month license renewal, a license is issued for what period and how many hours of continuing education are required?

a. one year and 12 hours of continuing education
b. 2 years and 24 hours of continuing education
c. 2 years and 30 hours of continuing education
d. 4 years and 36 hours of continuing education

Nevada State Specific-Standards of Conduct

224. If a man and his wife are the owner of real estate in joint tenancy, the kind of title or estate the wife would receive in the event of the death of her husband is a:

a. life estate
b. fee simple estate
c. dowcr interest
d. remainder estate

225. Title is conveyed to two persons who are NOT married, and no mention is made of how they are to take title. Title is presumed to be held as:

a. community property
b. tenants in common
c. joint tenants
d. tenancy in entirety

226. After the termination of all proceedings in connection with the judgment, a petition to collect from the Real Estate Recovery Fund must be filed within:

a. one year
b. three years
c. five years
d. seven years

227. A real estate broker is required to have all of the following EXCEPT:

a. trust account
b. day-to-day control of the business
c. use of the brokerage name in advertising
d. an acting manager at each branch office

228. Blind ads do NOT:

a. provide the name of the owner
b. provide the property address
c. give the listing price of the property
d. indicate that the advertiser is an agent

229. Brokers MUST keep records of transactions for a period of:

a. three years from the inception of a transaction
b. five years from the inception of a transaction
c. three years from the termination of the transaction
d. five years from the termination of a transaction

230. An agent decides to purchase a property through his or her broker's office. The earnest deposit must:

a. remain in the agent's checking account until the transaction closes
b. be placed in the broker's trust account
c. be placed in a neutral escrow depository in Nevada
d. be placed in the broker's operating account

231. A salesperson or broker advertising their own property must include one of the following in their advertisement:

a. office phone number
b. owner/agent
c. property address
d. legal description

232. Website advertising falls under the jurisdiction of the Real Division if the website:

a. offers real estate for sale
b. displays the name of a real estate company
c. collects an advertising fee
d. targets Nevada residents with the offering of a property interest

233. A real estate salesperson or broker may form a "team" or "group" to advertise and promote services if the team or group is comprised of:

a. real estate salespersons and mortgage brokers
b. real estate salespersons and/or broker-salespersons with the same brokerage
c. licensed agents from two or more brokerages
d. unlicensed assistants

234. A broker must review all contracts submitted through the broker's office within:

a. 3 days
b. 5 days
c. 7 days
d. 10 days

235. An ad prepared by a licensed salesperson promoting a broker's listing running in the local paper must include the:

a. salesperson's name
b. designated broker's name
c. brokerage name
d. brokerage telephone number

236. A broker's trust account:

a. may contain broker's personal funds
b. may be used to pay operating expenses
c. is subject to audit by Division representatives
d. must be bonded

237. When a salesperson receives earnest money, he or she should:

a. place it in his or her trust account
b. deposit it into the broker's trust account
c. keep his or her commission and give the balance to the broker
d. turn the earnest deposit over to the broker promptly

238. A buyer gives a post-dated check with an offer. The broker should:

a. wait to see if the check is good before presenting the offer
b. treat the check as any other check
c. inform the seller as to the form of the deposit
d. refuse to accept the offer until check is good

239. A broker for the seller is required to disclose to a potential buyer that:

a. the seller doesn't like the house
b. the seller is moving out of state
c. the seller is in poor health
d. a felony occurred on the property

240. A contract to be valid MUST:

a. be written
b. have notarized signatures
c. have parties 21 years or older
d. have acceptance of the offer

241. A purchase agreement must include:

a. the form of the earnest money deposit
b. notarized signatures of the buyer and seller
c. the proration settlement between buyer and seller
d. instructions on how title is to be taken

242. The Statute of Frauds is NOT applicable to a:

a. purchase contract
b. listing contract
c. lease for six months
d. deed

243. When a broker receives an offer of $51,500 for a property listed at $50,000, the broker should:

a. tell the seller it sold for $50,000 and keep the extra $1,500
b. present the offer and take a commission on $51,500
c. split the difference in the excess over $50,000.
d. tell the buyer the property is not worth $51,500

244. Equitable title under a purchase contract would refer to the:

a. seller's interest
b. buyer's interest
c. broker's interest
d. buyer and seller's interest

245. A buyer paid $3,000 for an option to purchase a house within 180 days for 4150,000. Within a month, the buyer made an offer to buy the house immediately for $130,000. Which of the following is true regarding this situation?

a. the seller may accept the offer for $130,000
b. the buyer is in default of the option agreement
c. both parties are in default of the option agreement
d. the option money is forfeited

246. "B's" offer to buy "S's" house has been accepted, but the actual sale will not take place for two months. Until that time, their written purchase contract is considered:

a. executory
b. voidable
c. conditional
d. pending

247. A contingency in a purchase contract is:

a. a statement making time of the essence in the performance of the contract
b. the seller's promise to prove clear title to the buyer's satisfaction
c. something that must happen before the buyer can be required to complete the purchase
d. a listing of personal property that is to be left by the seller

248. A seller receives an offer to purchase and puts forth a counteroffer to the purchaser. Until the purchaser notifies the seller of his or her acceptance or rejection, the seller:

a. may produce a new counteroffer
b. cannot accept another offer from a different buyer
c. may accept the buyer's original offer
d. is legally bound to the terms of the counter offer

249. When a contract contains provisions detailing what money would be levied against a party that refuses to perform, the amount specified is known as:

a. specific performance
b. consideration
c. liquidated damages
d. earnest money

250. A builder purchased a lot that had a very low down payment which he intended to pay off after he built and sold a house. He intended to obtain a construction loan to cover his building costs. The loan for the lot most likely had a:

a. release clause
b. maintenance clause
c. subordination clause
d. subrogation clause

251. Real estate title information is BEST found in the records of the:

a. Secretary of State
b. County Recorder
c. Tax Assessor
d. vendor

252. Under RESPA responsibility for the delivery of a good faith estimate of settlement costs rests with the:

a. buyer
b. lending institution
c. selling broker
d. escrow company

253. All of the following statements regarding a real estate closing statement are correct, EXCEPT:

a. the broker is responsible to review the closing statement
b. a preliminary closing statement is not required to be presented to the parties to the transaction before the day of closing
c. the closing statement is usually prepared and delivered by the escrow agent
d. the broker is responsible to answer any questions from the buyer or seller about the statement or any of the statement entries

254. To be depreciated, real property MUST be:

a. owned in fee simple
b. owner-occupied residence
c. paid for
d. improved

255. A broker has just received a full price offer on one of her own listings. Minutes later, she receives an identical offer from another office. The broker should present the offers:

a. in the order they were received
b. at the same time
c. in order received, but inform the owner about the duplicate offer
d. with the recommendation of acceptance of the first offer and the second to serve as a backup offer

256. An owner offers property on an "as is" basis. If the owner's agent has knowledge of a latent defect, the agent and owner MUST:

a. disclose the defect
b. repair the problem
c. maintain confidentiality
d. back out of the pending sale

257. If upon receipt of an offer to purchase under certain terms the seller makes a counter offer, the prospective purchaser is:

a. relieved from the original offer
b. bound to accept the counter offer
c. bound by the agent's decision
d. bound by the original offer

258. After a seller makes changes on the buyers offer to purchase, the salesperson should:

a. take all copies for signature by the buyer and promise to return a signed copy to the seller
b. leave a copy with the seller and take the others to be signed by the buyer
c. leave a copy with the seller as the final contract
d. leave a copy with the seller and promise to bring back a copy of the signed contract

259. A bank that requires that title insurance be obtained from a particular provider is a violation of:

a. Code of Ethics
b. Federal Fair Housing Act
c. Equal Credit Opportunity Act
d. Real Estate Settlement Procedures Act

260. A deed in lieu of foreclosure conveys title to which of the following:

a. lender
b. borrower
c. trustee
d. mortgagor

261. Under Nevada law the trust deed conveys the power of sale to the:

a. trustor
b. trustee
c. beneficiary
d. lender

262. Unless otherwise specified, a broker is required to deposit earnest monies in escrow or a trust account:

a. upon the buyer's acceptance
b. upon seller's acceptance
c. promptly
d. within 72 hours of receipt

263. The money that the salesperson receives from the buyer as an escrow deposit should be:

a. given to the seller
b. deposited in the salesperson's account
c. promptly turned over to the broker
d. immediately deposited in the broker's trust account

Nevada Sate Specific-Agency/Brokerage

264. When a broker misappropriates funds, it is called:

   a. conversion
   b. commingling
   c. conveyance
   d. consideration

265. An exclusive right to sell listing is an:

   a. executory implied contract
   b. executory bilateral contract
   c. executed bilateral contract
   d. executed implied contract

266. Oral testimony about a contract covered by the Statute of Frauds can be accepted as evidence for each of the following EXCEPT:

   a. explaining the written contract means other than stated
   b. clarifying an ambiguity
   c. showing fraud induced the contract
   d. showing a modified written agreement

267. A valid contract could be unenforceable because of the:

   a. lack of contractual capacity
   b. statute of limitations
   c. absence of consideration
   d. illegal purpose

268. An offer to purchase becomes a binding contract between seller and purchaser when the:

   a. seller has accepted the offer to purchase
   b. purchaser has signed the offer to purchase
   c. buyer has been notified of the seller's written acceptance of the offer to purchase
   d. broker accepts the earnest money deposit

269. A transaction is closed on February 15 and the buyer does not record the deed until April 24 of the same year. A judgment for $13,000 is filed against the grantor on April 21 of that year. The judgment is:

   a. a lien against the property
   b. invalid against the property
   c. a judgment inchoate
   d. a judgment reversion

270. When the Broker is absent from his or her business, all of the following are true, EXCEPT:

a. a designated office manager must be named by the broker
b. the designated office manger must be a real estate broker-salesperson
c. a designated office manager must be named when the broker will be absent for 15 days
d. the designated office manager must have two years' active experience in the last 4 years

271. A salesperson is the representative of the:

a. seller
b. buyer
c. broker
d. corporation

272. A salesperson can be compensated for an act within the scope of the real estate law by:

a. another salesperson
b. his or her broker
c. another broker
d. his or her principal

273. In the event that two brokers claim a commission under an open listing, the commission should go to the broker who:

a. listed the property
b. advertised the property
c. was the procuring cause of the sale
d. obtained the first offer

274. A commission is earned by a broker when the:

a. escrow is paid
b. funds are disbursed at settlement
c. broker finds a ready, willing and able buyer
d. seller is paid

275. Commission sharing is an agreement between:

a. broker and seller
b. broker and buyer
c. two salespeople within an office
d. cooperating brokers

276. A contract in which a property owner employs a broker to market the property, creates an agency relationship between the following:

a. buyer and seller
b. buyer and broker
c. broker and seller
d. broker, seller and buyer

277. Nevada statutes require that an exclusive listing contract include the:

a. street address
b. annual taxes
c. mortgage balance
d. expiration date

278. The commission amount is determined by:

a. local custom
b. multiple listing services
c. Real Estate Division
d. Negotiation

279. The collection of a commission from both parties to a transaction by the broker is:

a. prohibited by the Administrative Code
b. unethical
c. legal with full disclosure to both parties and with their written consent
d. illegal

280. Salesperson "T's" listing sells and is scheduled for closing in two weeks. Salesperson "T's" broker, "J" receives disciplinary action from the Real Estate Commission for a prior act and has the license suspended:

a. "J" and "T" are not entitled to a commission
b. "J" is not entitled to a commission, but salesperson "T" is
c. "J" and "T" will be entitled to the commission if "J's" broker license is reinstated
d. "J" and "T" are both entitled to a full commission

281. To collect a commission in court, a licensee MUST prove the:

a. listing was in effect at the time of closing
b. purchase contract was approved by the broker
c. licensee was licensed when the claim was made
d. listing was signed by the broker

282. When an agency relationship has ended, any confidential information learned during the relationship is:

a. considered immaterial
b. part of the MLS database
c. still confidential
d. shared with other clients

283. Which of the following is NOT true:

a. the listing must show a definite expiration date
b. an exclusive agency permits the seller to sell without liability to pay a commission to the broker
c. in an open listing the broker or salesperson that is the procuring cause receives the commission
d. net listings are illegal in Nevada

284. Upon obtaining a listing, the salesperson should advise the seller that the:

a. brokerage fee cannot exceed 6%
b. sale cannot be guaranteed
c. brokerage fee cannot be negotiated
d. listing must have a six month term

285. Mr. Smith is a tenant under a percentage net lease on commercial property. When the owner sells the real estate to a new buyer who plans to occupy the property, Mr. Smith's lease is:

a. canceled
b. still binding and Smith continues to pay rent to the original owner
c. still binding and Smith pays rent to the new owner under the terms of the original lease
d. subject to restructuring by the new owner

286. An authorization to sell is a mutual agreement between the broker and the principal and it is considered to be:

a. a contract for sale
b. a contract for personal and professional services
c. a contract for purchase
d. an exclusive listing

287. An exclusive right to sell agency could NOT be terminated prior to the expiration date when the:

a. agency is coupled with an interest
b. owner unilaterally declares the agency ended
c. principal dies
d. agent becomes incapacitated

288. A broker with an open listing can help protect her commission by:

a. notifying the other brokers in the area of her prospect's name
b. notifying the owner in writing that she is negotiating with a particular prospect
c. notifying the prospect that any purchase must be made through her
d. registering her prospect with the local real estate board.

289. To collect a commission under an exclusive right to sell listing, it is NOT necessary for a broker to prove:

a. the listing was signed by the seller
b. the broker was the procuring cause
c. the listing was valid
d. the broker was licensed at the time

290. A broker would be LEAST likely to advertise a(n):

a. exclusive agency listing
b. exclusive right to sell listing
c. open listing
d. listing for a rental with a purchase option

Nevada State Specific-Special Topic

291. Which of the following about a registered owner-developer is true:

a. must have a real estate license
b. must complete the 90-hour pre-licensing education
c. must hire a real estate broker-salesperson as the sales manager
d. owner-developer registration is good for two years

292. All of the following are correct about a subdivision advertisement, EXCEPT:

a. must be approved in writing by the Division
b. all press releases must be approved in writing by the Division
c. an approval number and developer's name must appear on the advertisement
d. modifications to approved advertisement must be submitted to the Division for approval

293. The maximum amount of money that may be paid from the Recovery Fund for any one licensee is:

a. $100,000
b. $75,000
c. $50,000
d. $25,000

294. A claim for money from the Recovery Fund could not be made by a:

a. buyer in a subdivision
b. seller of a residence
c. mortgagor
d. licensee

295. In Nevada, both ground and surface water:

a. are appropriated under the riparian doctrine
b. are appropriated under the littoral doctrine
c. belong to the public
d. belong to the federal government

296. All of the following are true for a domestic well, EXCEPT:

a. water right permit not required
b. pump age cannot exceed a daily maximum, of 1800 gallons
c. water cannot be furnished by a water district
d. subject to forfeiture or revocation

297. When altering a Nevada dry desert wash, a developer needs to consider the requirements of the:

a. CERCLA (Superfund)
b. Toxic Substance Control Act (TSCA)
c. Clean Water Act (Wetlands)
d. Superfund Amendments and Reauthorization Act (SARA)

298. A Brownfield is:

a. desert landscape
b. farmland that is not cultivated due to climate change
c. abandoned or underused urban area due to issues related to toxic contamination
d. large grassy area that has not been irrigated

299. All of the following are true about a clandestine drug laboratory, EXCEPT:

a. location for the manufacture of illegal substances, such as methamphetamine
b. meth labs can cause substantial damage to an owner's real property
c. meth labs are very hazardous and potentially explosive environments
d. disclosure that a property was the site of a crime that involved the manufacture of methamphetamine is a material fact that always must be disclosed

300. To manage a homeowner's association the manager must have all of the following, EXCEPT:

a. Community Manager Certificate
b. 12-months' experience managing a common-interest community
c. a real estate broker license
d. 60 hours of specified education

ANSWER KEY

Property

1. C Real estate is defined as: land plus improvements, buildings and other permanent attachments and appurtenances

2. A Indestructibility is a physical characteristic. The other physical characteristics of real estate are immovable and non-homogeneity. Improvements, scarcity and situs are economic characteristics of real estate.

3. C Non-homogeneity is a physical characteristic of real estate meaning that no two parcels of real estate are alike.

4. A Situs is an economic characteristic of real property meaning that value is enhanced by the desire of people to locate in a particular area.

5. B A fee simple estate is seldom, if ever, free of encumbrances.

6. B A defeasible estate or qualified fee is a freehold estate that can be terminated if certain conditions are not met.

7. A The purchase of the remainderman's interest in the property by the life tenant makes the life tenancy a fee simple absolute interest.

8. C The only interest that a grantor of a life estate could have is a reversionary interest.

9. D A fee simple estate is a freehold estate. Leasehold rights would be a leasehold estate.

10. B An estate in remainder is established when the grantor states in the deed that upon the death of the life tenant, the property will go to a third person.

11. B In order to grant an easement over the property a deed acknowledged by all of the owners would need to be delivered and recorded.

12. C Holding title as joint tenants provides the right of survivorship, which means that upon the death of one of the owners the survivors receive the decedent's interest without going through probate.

13. D Dying intestate means Alan did not have a will and since he also did not have any heirs the ownership of Alan's property passes to the state government under the government power of escheat. The death of Alan does NOT terminate the lease to Bruce so the state acquires the property subject to the lease rights of Bruce.

14. C Joint tenancy, which is more accurately referred to a joint tenancy with Right of Survivorship, requires the four unities of possession, interest, title and time. The unities can be remembered by the acronym PITT.

15. D Trade fixtures are items that are the personal property of a tenant or owner and used to carry on his or her business.

16. C An appurtenant easement is attached to the land and when the land is sold, the easement is transferred to the new owner; it is said to "run with the land".

17. C It is illegal to sell or transfer landlocked land meaning land without access, except for passing over another person's land. Since it is illegal to sell landlocked parcels, the owner will have to grant ingress and egress to the property, by granting an easement, known as an easement by necessity, for a road across the seller's property.

18. C The priority of liens, other than real property taxes and mechanic's liens, is determined by the order in which the lien is recorded.

Land Use Controls and Regulations

19. B The government's rights related to the limitation of private property rights are Police Power, Eminent Domain, Taxation and Escheat. Police power is the government's right to enact laws for the common good.

20. D Taking land for a parkway is the government's exercise of its right of eminent domain

21. B Restrictive covenants and deed restrictions are private limitations on land use. Zoning laws are an exercise of the government's police power and therefore a public land-use control. Assessments are considered a form of property tax.

22. B The taking of private property for public use after payment of compensation is the exercise of the government right of eminent domain.

23. A Laches is defined as the delay in asserting one's rights.

24. C A nonconforming use is a building or land use, which does not conform to the zoning ordinance. A nonconforming use is generally referred to as a "grandfather clause" when the building or land use was in existence prior to the adoption of the zoning ordinance.

25. C Down zoning occurs when a property zoned for higher-density uses is rezoned for lower-density uses.

26. B The special assessment is an involuntary specific lien.

27. A The homestead exemption is a legal life estate that protects an individual's primary residence from forced sale by creditors.

28. B Real property taxes are always in first lien position.

29. D Local associations adopt resolution that have to do with rules related to the REALTOR® members. The other answer choices are all methods for regulating land use by the government under its Police Powers.

30. B Restrictive covenants are private controls of land use.

31. C The collection of taxes is done under the governmental right of Taxation not Police Power.

32. B The taking of private property for public use after payment of compensation is the exercise of the government right of Eminent Domain.

33. B The process of taking private property under the right of Eminent Domain is known as Condemnation. The right is Eminent Domain and the process is Condemnation.

34. A The enactment of enforcement of zoning ordinances is based on police power.

Valuation and Market Analysis

35. C A licensee when taking a listing will generally complete a Comparative Market Analysis, which is a comparison of recent sales of similar properties in the area. This is the same approach as the appraiser uses when completing the market data approach.

36. B When the appraiser is computing the value using the Income Approach the operating income used should be the projected annual operating income. Therefore, the historical information received from the CPA should be adjusted for future expectations, such as rent increases or increased operating costs.

37. D It is generally believed that the estimate of the accumulated depreciation is more difficult to estimate than the cost of reproduction.

38. B Book value or net book value is an accounting term and it does not reflect current values, but is based on historical cost. Book value for income tax purposes is often referred to a tax basis.

39. B No two properties are identical and the appraiser must make adjustments to reflect the difference between the comparable sales and the subject property.

40. C The appraiser estimates the market value of a subject property. It is the appraiser's professional opinion of value.

41. B Rent control is the only choice that is political in nature. Rent control is not allowed in Nevada, but if it was it would be a political action and it would most likely have an adverse affect on values.

42. D Regression and progression exist when there are properties of different values in a neighborhood. Regression means that the better property is adversely affected by the poorer properties. Progression is the opposite.

43. B Remember the characteristics of value are: Demand, Utility, Scarcity and Transferability. Historical cost is not a characteristic of value.

44. B Economic life of an improvement is the estimated useful life of the improvement. The period during which the building contributes value to the land.

45. D The market data approach is the only possible approach that can be used for the valuation of vacant land. The income approach cannot be used since the land is vacant and there is no income. The cost approach cannot be used because you cannot build land.

46. B This procedure is known as Reconciliation. It was previously referred to as Correlation.

47. B When there have been few sales there is no data providing a current indication of value.

48. B Market value is described as an unemotional, objective price at which a seller would sell and a willing buyer would purchase, with neither party being under abnormal pressure to act.

49. B The assessment for property taxes seldom if ever has any indication of current values.

50. D The items in answer choices "a", "b" and "c" should NOT be considered when completing a current appraisal. The neighborhood forces outside the property can either affect the valuation positively or negatively. Negative forces outside the property itself are known as Economic Obsolescence and are generally considered to be incurable.

51. A The highest and best use is the most profitable use to which land can be utilized. It is that use which will bring the greatest return. After the appraiser determines the highest and best use, other factors to be considered in the valuation, such as project net income can be estimated.

52. D The proximity of a nuisance would be economic obsolescence, such as a nearby freeway.

53 D When a valuation of a property is made using the Income Approach to Value the calculation is a conversion of the projected operating income to a indicated market value using a capitalization rate.

54. B The gross rent multiplier is not an approach to value because the GRM is determined using the total rent potential of the property and therefore does not take into consideration any unusual expense that are unique to that property. The gross rent multiplier is an effective tool for a real estate agent when taking a listing for an income type property.

Financing

55. B The acceleration clause enables the lender to call the loan due and payable on default.

56. C A subordination clause allows the voluntary acceptance of a lower lien priority than the one to which the lien holder would otherwise be entitled.

57. B The mortgagor in a blanket mortgage would pledge more than one parcel or lot to secure the note. When a developer wishes to develop a large tract of land he or she would pledge all of the land as collateral with a release clause that the lender will, with partial payments on the loan, release the lot that has been sold so that clear title may pass to the lot purchaser.

58. C The power of sale clause is the right given to the trustee to hold a non-judicial foreclosure sale upon loan default and the request of the lender.

59. A The defeasance clause is a mortgage or trust deed clause that states the mortgage lien is defeated if the accompanying note is repaid.

60. B A wrap is created when the owner of a property has an existing loan on his property and a sizeable equity position. The owner allows the existing lien to remain in place, while selling the property for a higher amount. The buyer now makes payments on the new higher mortgage to the seller, who then makes the payment on the smaller first loan.

61. A The parties to a land contract, also known as a contract for deed or an agreement FOR sale, are the vendor (seller) and the vendee (the buyer).

62. B Usury laws establish the maximum rates of interest that can be charged. There is no longer a usury limit on real property loans.

63. D When real estate is acquired with the use of a land contract legal title passes to the vendee when the total obligation is paid.

64. A The graduated payment mortgage is a loan, which begins with low payments, but increases at regular intervals for a set number of years, then levels out for the balance of the term. The loan payments in the early years can result in negative amortization; meaning that the payment is not sufficient to pay the interest for the period. The unpaid interest is added to the loan balance; hence negative amortization.

65. C On a fully amortized loan with level monthly payments the amount of the payment allocated to interest decreases with each payment and the amount allocated to the principal reduction increases by the amount of the interest decrease.

66. B When the final payment is made on a loan secured by a trust deed, the beneficiary (lender) notifies the trustee that the loan has been paid and the trustee reconveys the naked title to the trustor. The document used to reconvey the naked title is the Deed of Reconveyance

67. B Regulation Z of the Truth in Lending Act applies to advertising the credit terms available in the purchase of a home. The only specific thing that may be stated in the advertising without making a full disclosure in the ad is the annual percentage rate spelled out in full. If any other specific credit terms are included in the advertisement, a full disclosure must be provided.

68. C An amortized loan is the most common real estate loan. This type of loan has a set payment of principal and interest that is calculated to pay the total interest and principal over the term of the loan.

69. D Regulation Z applies to advertising the credit terms available in the purchase of a home.

70. A A deficiency judgment is a judgment against the defaulting mortgagor for the

difference between the indebtedness and the sales prices through a foreclosure sale. The judgment is against the mortgagor, but available to the mortgagee.

71. A In participation loans lenders share in the net income of a project as additional interest on the loan.

72. B The trustee holds Naked Legal Title, which is also known as the Power of Sale Clause or Bare Legal Title.

73. D The FHA and VA loans cover single family residences and/or multi-family residences up to a four-plex, but the owner must occupy one of the units.

Laws of Agency

74. A The six components of a broker's fiduciary duty are loyalty, obedience, disclosure, confidentiality, reasonable care and diligence and accountability.

75. D The salesperson is a subagent of the employing broker and is therefore responsible to that broker.

76. B When a party allows an action to take place that would make a reasonable person believe that an agency relationship exists, estoppel agency precludes the party that allowed the action to take place from denying the relationship.

77. C Part of the fiduciary obligation is disclosure.

78. A The fiduciary duty of disclosure requires the agent to keep the seller informed and the obligation does not cease when the contract is in escrow.

79. D Making a profit at the expense of the agent's client is a violation of the fiduciary duty of loyalty. The courts have held over the years that in such a circumstance any profit must be paid to the client.

80. A Puffing is legal in Nevada, but it is discouraged because there is the potential that the exaggerated opinion could become a misrepresentation.

81. D An agent works with a customer and works for a client. In dual agency the broker works for both the buyer and the seller.

82. B Fraud or fraudulent misrepresentation is a deceitful practice or material misstatement known to be false and done with intent to deceive.

83. D The salesperson is an agent of the broker not the buyer. An agency relationship could be broker-buyer.

84. D Accepting compensation from both the buyer and the seller would create a dual agency relationship, which requires written informed consent from both parties.

85. B An agent has a responsibility to disclose to his/her client and is required to present all offers. The agent should also advise his/her client as to the agent's opinion of each offer.

86. A A universal or general agent must have a written document stating that he or she is an attorney in fact, which gives that individual the power of attorney.

87. A The actions of the salesperson indicate to the buyer that the agent is working for the buyer; hence implied agency.

88. B An exclusive agency would not create an agency by implication, but it would create a specific and expressed agency plus a fiduciary relationship with the owner.

89. C An exclusive right to sell listing requires the seller to pay the listing broker the agreed commission no matter who procures the buyer.

90. C The open listing is an agreement between the seller and the broker that requires the seller to pay that broker a commission only if that broker procures the buyer.

91. C Joe is due the full commission because Joe had an exclusive listing meaning no matter who procured the buyer the agreed upon commission was due Joe.

92. C Any multiple listing service is for member brokers who share information. Multiple listing services do not accept open listings, but they do generally accept exclusive right to sell and exclusive agency listings.

93. B In order to collect a commission there must be a valid listing contract between a licensed broker and signed by the seller; however, with an exclusive right to sell listing the broker does not have to prove that his/her efforts were the procuring cause.

94. A Commission rates are established through negotiations between the seller and the broker. Rates can vary between listings based on the negotiations and the nature of the agreed upon project.

95. D The listings need to be renegotiated since listings cannot be transferred to another entity without the seller's consent. If the broker had been a corporation and the father was the corporation's designated broker then the daughter could have been named the new designated broker and the listings would not need to be renegotiated.

96. D The fiduciary duty of a real estate agent does not include the providing of legal advice. In fact a real estate agent should not give legal advice, since to do so would be the unlicensed practice of law.

97. B A real estate salesperson can only be paid a commission by the broker with whom the salesperson is licensed.

98. A An agency relationship does not require an obligation to pay consideration.

99. B In a listing the seller is the Principal and the listing broker is the Agent.

Mandated Disclosures

100. D When the broker represents the owner of the property objectives of the seller should not be disclosed.

101. C The annexation in to the city is a material fact that could affect the consideration to be given and therefore must be disclosed.

102. B All parties to the contract must be informed of any material defect; even if it discovered after the contract has been formed.

103. C Environmental hazards are a material fact that must be disclosed to all parties to the transaction.

104. C Termite infestation and structural damage even if it has been repaired should be disclosed.

105. A The broker is required to inform the buyer about defects related to the property, which include the fact that the seller no longer likes the property. Normally the fact that a felony took place on the property would need to be disclosed, but a Nevada statute has made the discovery of that defect a responsibility of the buyer.

106. B The broker's statement about the zoning is a misrepresentation, which makes the agreement a voidable contract at the option of the buyer.

107. B Why the property is not desirable means to disclose any material fact that would adversely affect the consideration to be given by the prospective purchaser, which must be disclosed by the agent. The other items are considered confidential information and can only be disclosed with the permission of the seller.

108. A When the broker represents the owner of the property objectives of the seller should not be disclosed.

109. B The broker could be held liable under the theory that the broker is a professional and should investigate the accuracy of the seller's representation.

110. B Radon is a radioactive, colorless, odorless gas, which is produced when certain natural radioactive minerals break down or decay.

111. C The principal and the principal's agent have a duty to disclose known facts, which are not known to the other parties to the transaction and are not easily observable that materially affect the value of the property.

112. C A building containing asbestos is a material fact and must be disclosed to the seller and to any potential buyer.

113. C The proper disclosure by the seller of material facts is to be made in writing in a timely manner and in a format prescribed by the Real Estate Division; the Seller's Real Property Disclosure Form.

114. A The Seller's Real Property Disclosure Form must be completed by the seller at least 10 days before the escrow close.

115. D The buyer can only collect from the Recovery fund after obtaining a judgment against the seller and then only if the damages were caused by the actions of the licensee.

Contracts

116. C The acts described in a contract must be performed in a timely manner; meaning within the time limits established in the contract.

117. B A purchase contract that is formed is a binding contract and if one of the parties dies the beneficial interest and the obligations of the parties become an obligation of or benefit to the deceased's estate.

118. C The Statute of Frauds, which requires that contracts related to real property be in writing, was adopted to eliminate the false testimony under oath (Perjury) when oral contracts could be used to transfer real property.

119. B An executory contract for the purchase of real property generally refers to an agreement that is in escrow. During the escrow period the buyer has a contractual interest to receive legal title to the real property, which should be in a condition similar to when the contract was formed. This contractual interest of the buyer is known as equitable title.

120. D Novation means standing in the place of another or the substitution of parties.

121. B The offeror is the party making the offer. The offeree is the party receiving the offer and acceptance would be made by the party that received the offer.

122. B An option contract is a unilateral contract and the terms of the option are enforceable against the optionor, the one who grants the option.

123. C The parties to a contract must sign the agreement free of any threat or without duress. The party signing a contract under duress is said to lack capacity and that party can elect to void the agreement within a reasonable time after contract signing.

124. B Punitive damages are damages for a breach of contract that exceed the actual loss suffered.

125. D A contract requires competent parties, offer and acceptance, consideration and legal purpose and does not need to be written unless it is covered by the Statute of Frauds.

126. A Just like a check, numbers written as words prevail over the numerals.

127. C The contract is unenforceable because the agreement is void, since the offeror died before the contract was formed by the offeree's acceptance.

128. A Liquidated damages is a contractual provision for an agreed amount to be paid for damages in the event of a breach of contract.

129. A A void contract is an agreement that is NOT capable of enforcement because it does not exist as a contract. It is void because it does not have all of the elements required for legal enforcement as a contract.

130. B A contract signed by a 17-year old is voidable, since a 17-year old does not have contractual capacity.

131. A A lease for one year or less is not covered by the Statute of Frauds and can therefore be an oral agreement. An oral lease or rental agreement for six months is enforceable.

132. A The written lease is not enforceable because it has not been signed by both parties. The lease is a periodic tenancy on a month to month basis because the landlord has provided occupancy and the tenant has paid monthly rent that was accepted by the landlord.

133. C The landlord, also known as the lessor, is the owner of the property, who gives up the right of possession to the tenant, known as the lessee. Giving up the right of possession is the subordination of that right.

134. B A landlord has an obligation to reduce the damages when a tenant defaults on the terms of the lease. Mitigation means to reduce.

135. C Under an assignment of a lease the new lessee (the assignee pays the rent direct to the lessor; however, the assignor is responsible for the payment of the rent if the assignee defaults in its payment. The assignor's potential liability is known as contingent liability or secondary liability.

Transfer of Property

136. A Ownership of real estate is transferred by the delivery and acceptance of the deed. To transfer ownership of real property a deed does not need to be recorded, but to give constructive notice of the transfer it must be recorded.

137. D Dedication is the voluntary transfer of land by its owner for some public use. Dedication is voluntary alienation.

138. C If the unauthorized occupant of the land continues to occupy the land after the adverse user is ordered to desist by the owner, the occupation becomes even more hostile. The continuous use by the adverse claimant remains unbroken.

139. C A valid deed must name a definite grantee. A deed to Henry or Susan Smith is not definite; the deed must transfer the ownership to one of them or both of them, but not either of them.

140. A The party with the prior unrecorded deed and not in possession of the property will not be successful in claiming ownership and the right to occupancy of the property. The party in possession with a prior unrecorded deed will prevail over the present owner of record because the party is in possession. The tenant would be able to enforce the remaining nine months of the lease and the painter would be able to file a valid mechanic's lien.

141. A The habendum clause follows the granting clause in a deed and states the manner in which the property is to be held. The habendum clause literally means; to have and to hold.

142. B A special warranty deed offers the same covenants as a warranty deed except that they are limited to the period of time the grantor was in possession of the property. Defending the title against others who claim an interest through or

under her means limiting the defense to the period of time the grantor was in possession.

143. C If the unrecorded deed was found in Pete's house then it was not delivered and Pete still owned the house at his death. Pete's Will would cause the nephew to own the house.

144. B Adverse possession is the acquisition of title to real property through the unauthorized occupation of another person's land and meeting the requirements of open, hostile, notorious and continuous.

145. D The lender's policy is generally extended coverage, which includes a review of the public records (constructive notice) and an inspection of the property (actual notice).

146. A The earnest money that has been deposited in escrow reduces the additional funds that the buyer must deposit by the close of escrow. Any amount that reduces the amount of funds required from the buyer at closing is a credit to the buyer.

147. B RESPA requirements apply to loan transactions involving "settlement services" for federally related mortgage loans.

148. D The three-day right of rescission is available for residential mortgage loan refinancing and is provided for under the Truth in Lending Act.

149. C RESPA requires that a lender supply the HUD book entitled *Settlement Costs and You* and that a good faith estimate of settlement cost be supplied to the mortgagor within three business days.

150. D A valid deed MUST be delivered, but it does not need to be recorded.

151. A Signatures are always required by the grantor no matter what type of deed or how the grantee takes title. The grantee only must sign the deed when taking title as joint tenants or a married couple taking title as tenants in common.

152. B A single individual may exclude up to $250,000 of capital gain on the sale of his or her principal residence. The house must have been the taxpayer's principal residence for two of the preceding five years in order to qualify for the exclusion.

153. B The book value is the tax basis as it is the original cost plus any improvements less the accumulated depreciation. The gain is computed by subtracting the book value from the sales price.

154. D There is no statutory redemption period after a non-judicial sale.

Practice of Real Estate

155. B Advising a client how to take title to property is the unauthorized practice of law.

156. B A real estate commission is earned when the agent produces a ready, willing and able buyer; when the buyer and seller contract.

157. D A real estate salesperson can only be compensated by his or her employing broker.

158. B The broker is responsible for the actions of the salespersons employed by the broker and is required to supervise his or her licensed salespersons. The seller should have been informed that the check was postdated.

159. A The client is not required to accept an offer; however if the offer is exactly the same as the listing price and terms the broker could have a cause for action.

160. A The holder of the general power of attorney would have a conflict of interest when buying the property as he or she would be purchasing the property for his or her own benefit.

161. A Blockbusting is the illegal practice of inducing selling in a neighborhood for profit, based on the introduction of minority homeowners into a neighborhood.

162. C The Civil Rights Act of 1866 guarantees property rights to all citizens regardless of race.

163. B National origin is a protected class; marital status, credit history, and political affiliation are not classes protected by the Fair Housing Act.

164. D The 1974 amendments to the Civil Rights Act of 1968 added sex as a protected class; therefore the housing project directed to women is a violation of the Fair Housing Act.

165. C The Sherman Anti-Trust Acts are federal laws that condemn contracts, and conspiracies in restraint of trade.

166. D A real estate licensee has an obligation to deal fairly with all parties to a real estate transaction other than the client. The agent has a fiduciary obligation to the client.

167. D Commingling is the mixing of clients' or customers' funds with an agent's personal funds.

168. C Steering is the illegal practice of directing certain persons into or out of areas that are or are not integrated.

169. C The loss of the broker's license would not result from an action by the principal, but could result if an action was brought by the Commissioner. An action by the principal would not result in a fine or jail time, but could result in money damages.

170. A A broker must always disclose a material fact that could affect the consideration to be given by a party to the transaction.

171. A Conversion is the use of funds by the broker for other than their stated purpose.

172. D RESPA does not allow a seller of property to require a buyer to purchase title insurance covering the property from any particular title company as a condition of the sale.

173. A The broker is responsible for all acts of the licensed salespersons working for the broker. This responsibility includes the supervision of the agents; therefore the broker would be liable for the unethical conduct of a salesperson license with the broker.

174. C A broker is required to disclose to the seller any interest that the broker might have in the buyer. Lack of the disclosure generally results in the failure to succeed in any efforts to collect a commission on that transaction.

175. B Errors and omissions insurance protects real estate brokers and licensed salespersons from liability due to not meeting the professional standards of the real estate profession.

176. D A conditional acceptance means a counter offer. Any change whatsoever to an offer relieves the offeror of the original offer without exception. There is not a contract until there is offer, acceptance and notification of acceptance.

177. A The request by the offeree for more time does not automatically terminate an offer.

178. A The real estate agent should inform him that he may withdraw without penalty. An offer may be withdrawn at anytime before communication of acceptance.

Real Estate Calculations

179. C This is a gross rent multiplier application. The rent multiplier is computed by dividing the sales price of $132,000 by the gross rents of the duplex that was sold. The gross rents are $880 because the rent of $440 is per unit. The gross rent multiplier is 150 ($132,000 ÷ $880). The larger duplex rents for a total rental of $1,250 so its value is computed by multiplying the rent time the gross rent multiplier of 150. The indicated value is $187,500 ($1,250 × 150).

180. C The value decreased by $50,000 when the capitalization rate increased from 10% to 12%. Remember, when the capitalization rate goes up the value goes down.

181. B The loan amount is calculated by multiplying the sales price of $420,000 × the loan to value ratio of 80% ($420,000 × 80%).

182. B The loan balance outstanding before the February 1 payment created interest expense for the month of $500 so the annual interest is $6,000 ($500 × 12) and the loan balance is computed by dividing the annual interest by the interest rate of 10% resulting in the loan balance of $60,000 ($6,000 ÷ 10%). The $60,000 balance must be reduced by the principal reduction resulting from the February 1 payment. The reduction is $138 computed by subtracting the interest amount from the total payment; resulting in the February 2 loan balance of $59,862.

183. C First calculate the interest for the half year period by multiplying the loan amount by 7% and dividing the resulting annual interest by two. The total amount repaid equals the loan amount of $45,000 plus the interest for the one half year of $1,575.

184. D The buyer by assuming the loan will make the next payment that is due on July 1 and since interest is paid in arrears that payment will include the interest for the month of June. In the closing statement, the interest for the 12 days of June (day of closing belongs to the buyer) that the seller owned the property must be computed and charged to the seller. The buyer will obtain credit for the same amount because the buyer pays the total interest for the month and is reimbursed for the seller's portion in the closing statement.

185. A There are 43560 square feet in an acre of land; therefore five acres of land contain 217,800 square feet (43,560 × 5). If the five acres is being divided into six equal lots each lot will have 36,300 square feet (217,800 ÷ 6). The width of the lot is determined by dividing the 36,300 square feet by the known depth of 250 feet resulting in the answer of 145.2 feet.

186. C The legal description indicates that one and one quarter acres are to be paved, which converts to 54,450 square feet. The paving cost per square foot is $1.20 so the total paving cost is calculated by multiplying 54,450 by $1.20.

187. C Multiply the denominators of the fractions and divide 640 by the product of the multiplication process.

188. B The interest to be credited to the buyer is computed by multiplying the interest per day times the number of days the seller owned the property ($19.375 × 19 days). The answer of $368 is a credit to the buyer because the buyer pays the total interest for the month and is reimbursed for the seller's portion in the closing statement.

189. B The seller is to be charged with the amount of the rent that is paid for the period that the buyer will own the property (18 days) plus the security deposits. The information about the leases expiring and their need to be rewritten has no affect on the solution.

190. C The loan is based on the lower of the sales price or appraised value.

191. B The $70,500 that the owner wants to net represents 93% percent of the sales price computed by subtracting 7%, the commission rate, from 100%, the total. The answer is computed by dividing the $70,500 by the decimal equivalent of 93% or .93.

Specialty Areas

192. D The receipt of rebates or "kick backs" from the supplier would be a breach of the manager's fiduciary duty to the owner.

193. B Chattel is another name for personal property.

194. A These items are trade fixtures and Carl can remove the equipment installed before the lease expires.

195. C A property manager agrees to manage rental properties for the owner and for compensation. To accomplish the management responsibilities the manager must act in an ethical manner and the manager's fiduciary responsibility would

require the manager to have current knowledge of the rental rates and vacancies in the area.

196. D An annual budget could be required to be prepared, but the budget itself is not a typical part of the management agreement.

197. B Property management agreement requirements are not part of the landlord tenant act.

198. A A Landlord must give the residential tenant at least 24 hours, advance notice before entering the dwelling, unless an emergency necessitates immediate access.

199. B The owner determines the objectives.

200. A Technically, ownership in a condominium is individual fee simple ownership of a fractional interest, plus a share of the common elements and grounds of the property.

Nevada Sate Specific-Commission Duties and Powers

201. A The Real Estate Commission is composed of 5 members who are appointed by the Governor.

202. A The Real Estate Division is managed by the Administrator.

203. C Members serve 3-year terms with a maximum of two consecutive membership terms.

204. D A licensee is entitled to a hearing before Real Estate Commission before his or her real estate license can be suspended.

205. B The Real Estate Commission is composed of five members who are appointed by the Governor.

206. C A person who acts as a broker, broker-salesperson, salesperson, property manager or business broker without actually being licensed is subject to prosecution before any state court. The Real Estate Division may file the complaint.

207. B The Administrator heads the Real Estate Division on behalf of the Division of Business and Industry.

208. A The Administrator is appointed by the Director of the Nevada Department of Business and Industry.

209. C The licensee may be assessed an administrative fine in an amount not to exceed $10,000 for each violation.

Nevada State Specific-Licensing

210. B The corporation must designate one individual as the designated broker and the individual must be an officer of the corporation.

211. D The statute requiring licensure is adopted pursuant to the government's police power that allows the adopting of laws for the protection of the public.

212. D An attorney at law taking a listing is not the normal duty of a lawyer. It is in fact engaging in the activity of a real estate salesperson or broker.

213. D If license is not renewed it is a non-current license.

214. B A trustee in bankruptcy is a person acting under a court order and is specifically exempt from the licensing law.

215. B A licensed salesperson must work for a licensed employing broker.

216. B The license held for an individual working for a Broker is a broker-salesperson license.

217. B A licensed real estate salesperson does not need to be a resident of the state of Nevada.

218. C The showing of the house, its features and quoting prices to the public are activities that require licensing.

219. C An inactive renewed license indicates that fees to the Nevada Real Estate Division have been paid, but the license has been held, by the Division for more than 30 days.

220. B An original license for a real estate broker, broker-salesperson, or salesperson is for a 12-month period. During the initial 12-month period, a 30-hour post-licensing classroom course must be completed.

221. D New fingerprint cards are not required when submitting a Property Management Permit application.

222. A The signage must be erected and maintained in a conspicuous place and meet all of the same requirements of the main office.

223. B After the initial renewal, Nevada requirements for license renewal mandate 24-hours of continuing education for every 2-year license period.

Nevada State Specific-Standards of Conduct

224. B The husband and wife had a fee simple estate in the property and upon the death of her husband the wife owns the property in severalty with the same freehold estate that they owned together. A fee simple estate.

225. B In Nevada, two single people who do not address how they choose to hold title, will automatically become tenants in common.

226. A In order to collect from the Real Estate Recovery Fund action must be started within one years of the time the final judgment was issued, including appeals.

227. A A real estate broker is not required to have a trust account, unless the broker is involved in property management.

228. D A salesperson or broker acting as an agent shall not advertise property in a manner which implies that no salesperson or broker is taking part in the offer for sale, lease, or exchange. Such an advertisement is known as a Blind Ad.

229. D The broker is required to keep an original copy of the contracts in the brokerage files for a period of five years from the close of escrow (the termination of a transaction).

230. C The agent works for the broker so the earnest money deposit cannot be placed in the broker's trust account, as it would create a conflict of interest. The earnest deposit must be placed in a neutral escrow account and that account must be in Nevada.

231. B Any salesperson or broker advertising the salesperson's or broker's own property for sale, lease or exchange shall disclose the salesperson's or broker's status as a licensee and as the property owner.

232. D The use of electronic media, such as the Internet or web site technology, that targets Nevada residents with the offering of a property interest, constitutes the dissemination of advertising.

233. B A team or group must be comprised of real estate salespersons or broker-salespersons, all working for the same broker.

234. B The responsible broker must approve listings and purchase contracts within five days.

235. C The name of the brokerage is required to be included in any advertisement.

236. C The broker's trust account is subject to audit by a Real Estate Division representative.

237. D Nevada statutes require licensed salespersons to promptly turnover funds received to his or her broker.

238. C The seller must be informed of the post-dated check at the time the seller is considering the offer.

239. A The broker is required to inform the buyer about defects related to the property, which include the fact that the seller no longer likes the property. Normally the fact that a felony took place on the property would need to be disclosed, but a Nevada statute has made the discovery of that defect a responsibility of the buyer.

240. D There must be offer, acceptance and notification to have a valid contract.

241. A The form of the earnest money deposit MUST be included in an Real Estate Purchase Contract.

242. C A lease for one year or less is not subject to the Statute of Frauds.

243. B All offers are to be presented.

244. B The seller agrees to deliver ownership of the real estate and the buyer's interest is that the condition of title will be the same as when the contract is formed. The buyer's interest is known as equitable title.

245. A The option contract does not prohibit the buyer from making an offer for the seller to consider.

246. A An executory contract is one that has been formed, but the agreed upon acts have not been performed.

247. C An example of a contingency is the qualification of the buyer for the real estate financing that is needed to complete a purchase.

248. A The seller may produce a new counteroffer, can accept another offer from a different buyer, but may not accept the buyer's original offer because the counteroffer rejected it. No one is legally bound to an offer or counteroffer until there is a meeting of the minds.

249. C An example of liquidated damages is the acceptance by the seller of the earnest money deposit for damages, as specified in the contract, when the buyer defaults.

250. C The subordination clause allows the builder to obtain a construction loan. Construction lenders generally demand to be in first position, so the builder would require the seller of the lot to include a subordination clause in the lot purchase financing.

251. B Every state has adopted recording acts to allow every instrument or document by which an estate, interest or right in land is created, transferred or encumbered to be placed in the public record. Within each stat, each county has a public recorder's office that is located in the county seat.

252. B The lending institution is responsible for the delivery of a good faith estimate of settlement cost at the time of loan application or within 3 business days.

253. B A preliminary closing statement is to be provided to the buyer and the seller no later than the day before the closing.

254. D The depreciation calculation does not include the cost of land. The improvements to the land are the only portion of the total cost that is depreciated.

255. B The duty of loyalty to the client requires that the offers be presented at the same time.

256. A The fact that the property is being offered "as is" does not reduce the obligation to deal fairly with all parties to the transaction. Dealing fairly requires the disclosure of any known latent defects.

257. A The counter offer, sometimes referred to as a "contingent acceptance" relieves the original offeror of his or her offer.

258. B A copy of an agreement should always be left with a party to the agreement and the salesperson should not promise that the buyer will agree to the changes made by the seller.

259. D The Real Estate Settlement Procedures Act (RESPA) prohibits a lender from requiring that the title insurance be acquired from a specific title insurer.

260. A A Deed in Lieu of Foreclosure is used when a owner and lender do not want go through the time consuming and expensive process of foreclosure. The deed in lieu is not as damaging to the credit of the borrower as a foreclosure.

261. B The trustee holds the Power of Sale for the benefit of the lender.

262. C Nevada statutes require that the broker promptly deposit trust funds, into the trust account. Promptly means by the next business day.

263. C Nevada statutes require that a salesperson promptly turn earnest money deposits over to his/her broker or deposit into escrow CD upon acceptance.

Nevada State Specific-Agency/Brokerage

264. A Misappropriation is using funds for other than their intended purpose; conversion.

265. B A listing that is still in effect would be executory. An exclusive right to sell listing is a bilateral contract, as both parties to the agreement have made a contractual promise.

266. A The parol evidence rule establishes that the written contract is superior to an oral agreement and that the written contract will stand on its own. This means that where there is a written document that states that 100 acres of land is being sold oral testimony cannot be used to say that an oral agreement was reached that revised the written contract to cover 160 acres. Such oral testimony would not be accepted by the courts.

267. B Contractual capacity, consideration and legal purpose must be present for a contract to be valid. However, if the statute of limitations has run on a valid contract and a party attempts to enforce its terms the court action will no be allowed.

268. C There must be notification to the purchaser of the seller's acceptance of the offer in order to have a valid contract. Meeting of the minds.

269. A The grantor has sold the property before the date of the judgment, but the buyer of the property does not record the deed until three days after the date of the judgment. The public record still shows that the grantor owns the property and when the judgment is recorded it becomes a lien on all property that the public record shows as owned by the grantor.

270. C A broker shall not be absent from his or her business for 30 days or more if he or she is the only broker in his or her office unless he or she inactivates his or her license or otherwise notifies the Real Estate Division in advance.

271. C The licensed salesperson represents the Broker and is a sub-agent of the broker.

272. B A licensed salesperson is a representative of the Broker and can only be compensated by the Broker for any licensed activities.

273. C Procuring cause is the standard for determining who will receive a commission when two brokers claim a right to the commission.

274. C The commission is earned when the broker finds a ready, willing and able buyer; however the commission is seldom paid before the close of escrow.

275. D A commission sharing agreement is generally the provision in Multiple Listing Service arrangements where the listing broker agrees to pay the selling broker a portion of the total commission for bring a buyer. The brokers in this type of arrangement are known as cooperating brokers.

276. C A contract that employs a broker to market a property is a listing and it is between the seller and the broker.

277. D The statutes require that the expiration date be included in a listing contract. The other items, if they are applicable should be included, but they are not required by statute.

278. D The commission rate or amount is determined by negotiations between the broker and the seller.

279. C Nevada statutes require that the representation of more than one party in a real estate transaction may only be undertaken upon licensee's full disclosure to each party that he or she is acting for more than one party in that transaction and with each party's subsequent consent to multiple representation in writing. A Consent to Act form must be reviewed, considered, and approved or rejected by both parties to the transaction.

280. D The commission was earned by the broker and salesperson prior to the broker's suspension; therefore they can be paid their commission at the close of escrow.

281. C Prior to a court hearing, the court will require the plaintiff to prove that a valid real estate license was held when the commission was collected. The court action will be dismissed if the required proof cannot be provided.

282. C After the termination of the agency relationship all confidential information must still be treated with confidence.

283. D A net listing is discouraged in Nevada, but it is not illegal.

284. B In negotiating a listing the agent should not guarantee that the sale will be made.

285. C The lease does not terminate on the sale of the property by the landlord.

286. B A brokerage agreement is a contract for the employment of a broker. It is both a contract listing the property for sale and a contract for personal services between the broker and the seller.

287. A An agency coupled with an interest is more than a personal service contract. A seller may not unilaterally terminate a listing, without cause, when the agency is couples with an interest. An example of an agency coupled with an interest is when a broker pays on the seller's mortgage debt to avoid foreclosure.

288. B Notifying the owner documents that the licensee is the procuring cause.

289. B It is not necessary to prove that the broker was the procuring cause when there is an exclusive right to sell listing.

290. C A broker would not advertise an open listing because of there is no guarantee of earning a commission; any number of brokers could have an open listing with the seller.

Nevada State Specific-Special Topic

291. C A registered owner-developer must hire a real estate broker-salesperson as the sales manager. The owner-developer registration is good for one year.

292. B A press release is exempted from the approval regulations and need not be submitted to the Division for approval if no advertising fee will be charged and two other exemption requirements.

293. A The Real Estate Recovery Fund will have no more responsibility to pay losses resulting from acts of a licensee once the fund has paid $100,000 in damages caused by that licensee.

294. D A licensee acting as a principal or agent in a real estate transaction has no claim against the fund.

295. C Nevada statutes provide that all water within the boundaries of the state, whether above or beneath the surface of the ground, belongs to the public.

296. D The domestic well exemption is not subject to forfeiture or revocation, and a homeowner cannot be required to cease pumping as long as the domestic well is operating properly.

297. C The wetlands definition as interpreted by the EPA can apply to the filling or altering of Nevada's dry, desert washes or doing site work on lowland vegetated areas and altering artificial lakes and streams.

298. C A Brownfield is a property, the expansion, redevelopment, or reuse of which may be complicated by the presence or potential presence of a hazardous substance, pollutant, or contaminant.

299. D The fact that the property is or has been the site of a crime that involves a meth lab is not considered a material fact for a real estate transaction if either of the following is the case: (a) All materials and substances involving methamphetamine have been removed from or remediated on the property by an entity certified or licensed to do so; or (b) the property has been deemed safe for habitation by a governmental entity.

300. C The manager of a Common-Interest Community does not need a real estate broker license.